The Essential Pattern

Finding Our Cosmic Connection

Rosalind Thorp

Agents of Change
Columbus, North Carolina

This book is dedicated to my daughter

Anne Jacquetta Chalmers

The Essential Pattern

Library of Congress Cataloging-in-Publication Data

Thorp, Rosalind-1936–
      The essential pattern : finding our cosmic connection / Rosalind Thorp.
          p. cm.
      Includes bibliographical references (p.)and index.
      ISBN 1-928992-03-x (alk. paper)
      1. Astrology. I. title.

      BF1708.1 .T496 2001
      133.9'3--dc21

2001022495

Original artwork by Rosalind Thorp
Computer preparation of artwork: Rochelle Sellers
Editors: Brian Crissey and Pamela Meyer

Printed in the United States of America.

For a free catalog and a sample of *The 5th World Journal*, write to
Agents of Change
P. O. Box 1429
Columbus, NC 28722
U.S.A.

or log onto http://5thworld.com.

Agents of Change is an imprint of Granite Publishing, LLC,

Contents

Foreword

"I looked at the foxgloves and the beautiful birches, and thought—each year the flowers come back; the leaves return when they should, and as they should again and again.... They follow the same genetic code, but they are not the same flowers or leaves. They represent a very similar pattern of energy and seem the same. Year after year they return faithfully as the seasons pass.

"Energy is trapped in the foxglove seeds and conforms to a pattern. It is a residual energy pattern and connects with a cycle. Humans, too, are linked with cyclical patterns and 'return.' This is what is meant by reincarnation—energy return in physical form."

Sometime in 1987 I began writing a few sentences. They came into my mind in brief statements and short paragraphs that explained and expanded their meaning. I felt a compelling urgency to record them. At first, I often pulled my car to the roadside to capture the words which rushed into my mind. Later, I was able to harness the inflow. I became aware that I was being channeled.

Most of the information in this book has been channeled by energies that involved me in different disciplines. My contribution has been in putting the subject matter together in the form in which it is presented. In particular, I hope that the astrological insights will enlighten many misconceptions about the subject. Although I have been fascinated by astrology for many years, the astrological content has been kept to a minimum in the book. For those who wish to know more, I refer them to the vast amount of wonderful material already written.

When I was first introduced to astrology, it was like any other new subject. Not long after serious study, I realized that if one had a birth chart (natal horoscope) so, also, would there be a death chart, and that a death chart was as much a part of our life as our birth chart. From that moment I changed my whole perspective of life on this planet. About five years later, intensive channeling began.

Writing a book is a way of sharing thoughts with others. I wish to share these thoughts with you as we examine an energy other than heat, light, electricity, magnetism, sound, gravity.

This interdisciplinary work is offered at a time of growing awareness that fundamental changes are occurring in society.

—Rosalind Thorp

Introduction

Thesis Outline

An energy exists: unseen…untouched…ubiquitous.

This book portrays, in new perspective, a theme that pervades all cultures: the belief in an intangible common link among all things that has been sensed from ages past, but never quite identified. The link is cosmic energy.

The thesis considers the cosmos, including man and his actions, in terms of multi-dimensional energy patterns in motion, and existence in terms of these patterns. It shows that nothing is without an energy pattern, that these patterns are essential energy units and that cosmic energy, which flows through a network of cosmic body alignments, links all things through pattern interconnection.

The theme is concerned with arrangement: the architecture of energy pathways which occur as cosmic bodies orbit. It shows that energy pattern relationships are responsible for everything that happens; that an energy process intensified by the moon causes everything to be the way it is on earth; that cosmic energy moves into space; that time does not exist without energy; that there is an order, or universal sequence, so that everything occurs through a process of synchronicity. It states that nothing happens by chance and insists that everything is significant. It emphasizes the need to consider cycles, showing that all things are cyclical because the nature of cosmic energy itself is cyclical. Through energy cycles, it shows that cosmic energy is a continuum which allows the phenomenon of energy return, which explains why history is similar from time to time, yet never quite repeats itself. It discusses birth, death and the life cycle and examines the deeper meaning of existence, including non-physical reality, as it leads the reader through concepts of time and space.

Metaphor

For all of us life is a journey—a passage through space. Like a footstep, each moment is as necessary as the one before and the one to come—each to be lived in its entirety to completion before the next, each dependent upon the preceding one and preparing for the next…continuous. As a clock ticks and marks the time of day, as the planets move in the heavens and mark positions in the cosmos, so we move in our timespace.

Everything has a lifepath, a destiny, or karmic program to follow, where events are not only timed to the fraction of a second, but also occur in exact sequence. Each lifepath is uniquely ours and belongs to a vast universal energy system. The idea of a pre-ordained destiny for each of us is a belief held by many cultures. The comprehension of it in terms of energy patterns approaches this ancient concept in a new way.

The universe is an energy system. That this efficient and powerful system is constantly operating for each of us, connecting and disconnecting our lives with others and with events, is overwhelming, but it does exist. It is a cyclical rhythm of forces in keeping with cosmic laws.

Respect For The Earth

In the past, humans lived in harmony with cosmic forces. We observed the vast rhythm of life, obeyed its laws and knew our place, even if we did not comprehend the physics of the mechanism. Modern society has lost touch with the harmony of nature. Through the misuse of energy, the whole network is suffering because so many individual units are in disarray. Not until respect for the earth is fully acknowledged will harmony begin to replace discord. Respect is the prerequisite which must precede the change.[1]

Astrology

Astrology is the study of cosmic body movements in relation to events on earth.

Ancient man correlated human behavior and events on earth with cosmic configurations and found an association with heavenly bodies. From simple cosmic observation, astrology evolved into a comprehensive interpretation of complex phenomena derived from stellar arrangement, in particular, planetary configurations. Although modern astrology has the advantage of rapid computer calculations, the full meaning is still dependent on accurate human analysis and interpretation. Comprehension may be compared to the difference between translation and interpretation of a language. What is written in the cosmos may be translated into an astrological chart: a cosmic energy pattern. The interpretation gives meaning to it.

Many texts consider astrology in detailed specifics rather than concepts. This leads the reader into the mind-boggling realms of the professional astrologer, where a lack of sufficient study and full comprehension often cause frustration and rejection of the subject. This study acknowledges astrology which is presented in a particular way and provides the framework for part of this work. It is written at a time of universal need for rethinking and re-evaluation. The thesis refers to astrology to describe energy patterns which form, interact, and re-occur in a continuum of energy cycles.

Human difference is well accepted. That an energy pattern determined by the stars contributes to individual uniqueness is less readily acknowledged. In fact, everything is associated with an energy pattern: cities, automobiles, trees in the forest, the forest itself, a hockey team, a coat, a cat, even a crystal! It is how we are linked to the cosmos.

It is time, then, to reconsider astrology—to take another look at the stars and the energy emanating through the cosmos, to examine the influence of that energy on our lives. In different ways and at different times, we all feel cosmic energy.

We sense something, but what is it?

---

1. See "Neptune's Revenge" on page 67.

One • Cosmic Energy

Invisible…intangible…yet sensed….

A force exists which holds everything together like a universal glue and causes all things to occur. This force depends on the motion of cosmic bodies and their emissions.

All cosmic bodies are energy sources. The sun as a source of energy is familiar, particularly in the form of heat and light. What is less well known, less understood, and less readily accepted, is the effect of the sun in relation to all other bodies, particularly the planets and asteroids within the solar system.

Each cosmic body is a center from which specific energy is emitted so that each is associated with particular influences. In astrological terms these influences are known as energy principles; specific principles have specific effects. In this way each cosmic body has a particular effect on Earth. For example, an energy principle of Saturn is restriction. In everyday life the effect of this influence is felt as control, or limitation.

When two or more cosmic bodies are linked together in a particular angular relationship, a specific energy principle exists for the combination. This means that in combination, the effect of primary principles is modified. Since cosmic bodies are always in motion, different links continually occur making cosmic configuration a crucial factor in determining the energy influence. Consequently, pure principles are less in evidence. Energy principles are most commonly experienced as a combined effect with a dominant influence. These cosmic body emissions combine to produce the underlying force in the universe. These emissions, or cosmic energy, may be described as the connective tissue in the cosmos: the common intangible bond among all things. Its elusive nature may be attributed to the constantly changing arrangement of energy directions which link Earth with the cosmos.

Cosmic energy involves alignments among focus points: energy sources in the cosmos and different locations on Earth. Alignments among cosmic bodies and Earth create energy pathways which allow energy to flow in particular ways. These pathways, or energy directions, form an angular network of geometrical shapes. A physicist would use vector diagrams to illustrate their structural nature. These energy-defined shapes in space are determined by cosmic configuration. As orbital motion rearranges the cosmos, changing alignments cause different positions on Earth to come into focus. When energy directions change, different energy shapes come into existence. Different energy principles begin to have an influence. The effects on Earth change.

Cosmic energy is associated with angles. These angles are important because they affect the energy influence. With some exceptions, the orb of influence is five degrees. Cosmic body positions are, therefore, very significant.

Cosmic energy is always an arrangement of energy principles.[1] Associated with its influence and known by its effect, what is observed is the outcome of its expression. Essentially, cosmic energy may be pictured as constantly changing energy co-ordinates. The concept is of momentary shapes—invisible structures created by energy pathways.

CONCEPT: Shape is integral to cosmic energy processes.

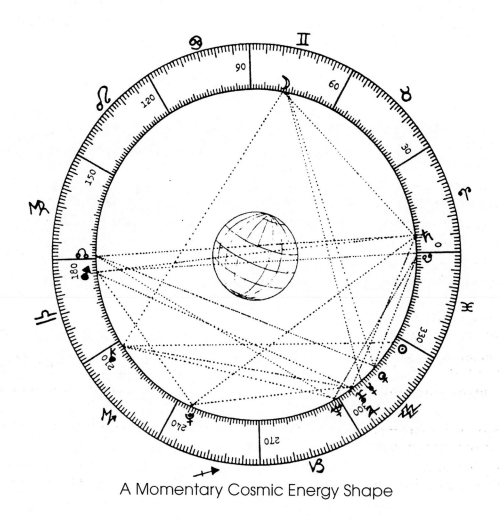

A Momentary Cosmic Energy Shape

In February 1997 the moon in transit travelling through the sign of Gemini made aspects to the various cosmic bodies in the following order: Chiron, Saturn, Mars, Pluto, Jupiter, Uranus, Mercury, Venus, sun, Neptune, and moon's nodes. As cosmic energy links occurred, different momentary shapes came into existence. The shape shown is the angular relationship of bodies in the cosmos at the time of the Jupiter/Uranus alignment calculated for 9:23 P.M. EST., Washington, D.C.[2]

1. See "Suggested Reading," *The Combination of Stellar Influences,* Ebertin, page 203.
2. See *The Mountain Astrologer,* Dec/Jan 1996-97, page 15.

Body in Cosmos

Earth

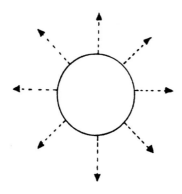

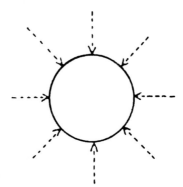

Specific energy emanates from each body

In constant reception of cosmic energy

Crystalline Concept

Cosmic energy defines shapes.

Cosmic energy not only surrounds all things on Earth, but like the human aura is constantly changing its shape. When we look at someone we see another person, a physical body. We do not see the surrounding energy because it is invisible to most of us. This energy links the individual to the cosmos. These links are energy directions which form geometric shapes by defining spaces. If this energy were visible, and could be momentarily captured as in a photograph, we would see that everything exists within a shape, similar to a crystal.[3]

Crystals are strictly organized structures. The most important feature common to all crystals is the regularity of the atomic structure. It is like a scaffolding of geometrically arranged atoms in which there are regular spaces among the support system. The regularity permits energy to flow in particular ways, as the wind is funneled through mountain valleys or parallel city streets.

The Earth is an energy environment—a space filled with cosmic energy directions which interconnect at angles. It may be likened to a lattice where the framework forms the cosmic energy pathways or channels, much like the arrangement of energy axes in a crystal.

CONCEPT: All things exist within geometric shapes formed by energy directions.

---

3. See "All Things Exist In A Cosmic Energy Shape" on page 4.

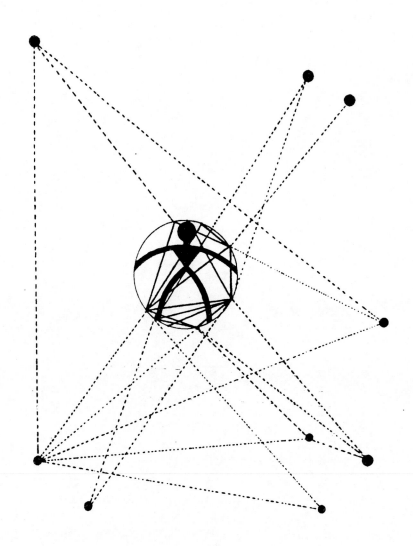

All Things Exist In A Cosmic Energy Shape

We live in the shape of our internal energy directions. This shape is constantly bombarded by cosmic influences in the form of external energy directions.[4]

The diagram shows the concept of cosmic energy directions surrounding an individual. As orbital motion changes cosmic body positions, the external energy shape changes. As the shape of energy changes, the energy influences also change. A different effect occurs.

---

4. See "Sensitive Points" on page 19; "Internal Energy Directions" on page 19; and "Crystalline Concept" on page 21.

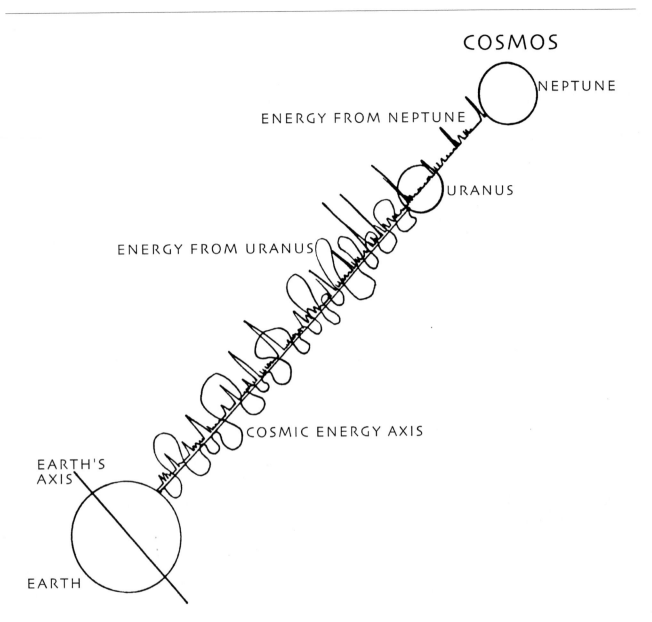

Cosmic Energy Axis

This illustration shows a cosmic energy axis. The Uranus/Neptune conjunction in Capricorn in 1993 is selected for the diagram. Energy from both planets forms an energy path to Earth for a considerable period because the planets move so slowly. A cosmic energy axis is to be differentiated from a theoretical axis around which a rotating body turns.

Fibre Analogy

Cosmic energy exerts its influence through focus points.

Cosmic energy directions are like threads of energy fibres between focus points—bodies in the cosmos and energy codes on Earth. With approaching alignment, the power of cosmic energy strengthens in the way that a rope becomes taut, causing a hold until alignment, then suddenly weakens as alignment is released. Lunar movement intensifies the energy influence, which has its effect as it builds in strength. The effect changes as cosmic bodies rearrange themselves and create different links.

Cosmic links may be fleeting or more prolonged. Lunar links, which form and release quickly account for daily activity. Their influence is brief. When a cosmic link exists for a long time, as from a very slowly moving planet such as Neptune, it behaves like a shaft, an axis around which other energy directions revolve. The influence may last for two years or longer.[5,6] The effect is far reaching and long lasting.

The nature of orbital movement is such that a cosmic body, and therefore, its energy influence, returns to each point of its orbit in repeated succession. The frequency of return to any given position, or one complete cycle, is known as the cyclical interval. Each cycle is a cosmic energy pulse. Each pulse is a part of cosmic rhythm.[7]

Throughout each year as the Earth revolves around the sun, all things on Earth experience a different position in the orbital path. In each position, the Earth experiences a particular relationship with the sun. At each orbital point, all other cosmic bodies are also in different positions relative to the Earth. This means that the Earth encounters a continually changing relationship with all other cosmic bodies. As the Earth rotates on its axis, each point on Earth is thus exposed to the prevailing pattern of cosmic influences.

Since cosmic forces on Earth are dependent on orbital motion, they are, therefore, linked to the cycles of cosmic bodies and ultimately controlled by them.

CONCEPT: Cosmic energy is a cyclical continuum.

Cosmic energy conforms to the principle of impermanence. The concept is a momentary expression in physical reality in which nothing lasts forever.

---

5. See "Cosmic Energy Axis" on page 5.
6. See "Uranus/Neptune Conjunction: 171-Year Cycle" on page 69.
7. See "Cosmic Rhythm" on page 75.

Cosmic energy links all things together.

The whole world shares cosmic energy. Whether it manifests in human form, a flower, or a rock, cosmic energy is represented in everything according to a code that is determined by a cosmic configuration at a particular time. Although each cosmic body is represented in each code, the arrangement determines which energy principles will predominate. Cosmic energy codes, termed energy patterns in this thesis, are like codes which inhabit a computer that are activated only by a specific connection. Each cosmic code, or pattern, is unique. In this way each responds differently to the same circulating cosmic energy. Cosmic links to common energy sources bring to the fore the concept of the unity among all things. Through common energy principles, everything is connected together in a myriad of ways.

Thus, arrangement is the essential component of cosmic energy, making configuration more important than the energy itself. It acknowledges the design principle of how everything fits together. It is the analogy of a heap of stones and rocks, commonly referred to as rubble. Within the heap the potential exists for wonderful arrangements, but requires a design.

Cosmic energy exists within the universe in a similar way.

Two • The Natal Pattern

Cosmic motion

A cosmic energy pattern describes an arrangement of cosmic bodies. Each arrangement determines the energy principles within the pattern and, in turn, the nature of its behavior. Cosmic energy patterns form through the movement of cosmic bodies. Although a cosmic pattern exists at all times, it changes constantly because cosmic bodies are always in motion and, therefore, rearranging themselves. Cosmic motion allows new patterns to come into existence. Each pattern is momentary.

Any position on Earth is always geometrically relative to the positions of cosmic bodies and is a focus point for incoming cosmic energy. At all times the energy focused through an Earth position is determined by the prevailing cosmic configuration. In this way each Earth position receives a particular pattern of cosmic body emissions at a particular moment in time. As each birth occurs, it associates itself with the prevailing cosmic configuration. Termed a natal pattern in this book, it is known astrologically as a natal chart and reflects a map of the cosmos at the moment of birth in the place where the individual is born. Not only is a birthplace a position on Earth, it is also a position in the universe, for all things are in motion, including the solar system itself. For this reason, the exact time and place of birth are very important to each individual. It is at birth that the energy directions from all over the universe are imprinted on the individual.

Although natal pattern similarities exist because the prevailing cosmic configuration imprints each Earth position in a particular way at a particular time,[1] no two natal patterns are exactly the same because the cosmos is in a constant state of flux: everything is moving relative to everything else. Even identical twins have a slightly different cosmic imprint because each has different ascendant and mid-heaven points.[2]

Thus, it is movement, the spinning Earth within the motion of the cosmos, that gives natal patterns their infinite variety and uniqueness.

Representation

In this book cosmic energy patterns are represented diagrammatically, in an artistic way, or in technically accurate astrological charts. Charts, or cosmic maps, may be calculated to show the positions of the cosmic bodies relative to the reference point in time and interpreted in astrological terms.

---

1. Compare all October 7th birthdays in a single year in a large city.
2. With the exception of astro twins, see "Suggested Reading" on page 203.

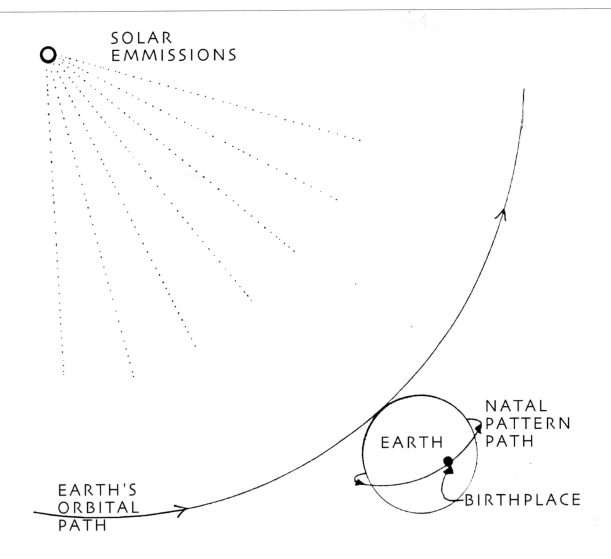

SOLAR
EMMISSIONS

EARTH'S
ORBITAL
PATH

EARTH

NATAL
PATTERN
PATH

BIRTHPLACE

Every twenty-four hours a birthplace rotates once with the Earth in the daily cycle, and slowly travels round the sun as the Earth makes its yearly cycle. Within this period, all other cosmic bodies also change position, thus creating the opportunity for an infinite number of different patterns.

A cosmic configuration is an energy arrangement.

Every morning the world wakes up to a different cosmic configuration which changes slightly throughout the day and night. Each arrangement which occurs takes its place in a sequence of cosmic patterns. The process is cyclical. It is also multidimensional, since each pattern is linked to much slower, and more complex, cosmic energy cycles of relationship and position spanning millennia.[3] At any time the prevailing cosmic energy arrangement, which affects everyone and everything, may become the natal pattern for someone or something. Not every cosmic pattern which forms is captured in physical reality as a natal

3. See "Suggested Reading" on page 203: *Astrological Timing,* Dane Rudhyar.

pattern. Each birth captures an energy arrangement so that a new birth is as important for contributing a different energy pattern to Earth as the natal pattern is to the new physical being, or the inception of any new thing.

Cosmic Code

For all things on Earth, the natal pattern is the most important energy pattern.

The newborn is like a new computer terminal which has yet to be programmed. Each individual program begins at birth.

At the moment of birth, the newborn is analogous to an old-fashioned, uncut gramophone record waiting for sound. As the Earth spins on its axis, the newborn goes round like a new disc, and picks up the cosmic energy vibrations as an inscriber records sound. In this way, from the moment of birth, the newborn is exposed to cosmic energy from all sources in the universe. The natal pattern is imprinted and established. It is the beginning of individuality.

Each natal pattern represents an arrangement of cosmic energy which, in turn, defines a shape or aura around the person or thing it describes. In this description is a specific identification, like a fingerprint, a unique code which links the individual to the cosmos. In this way everyone and everything may be identified with a particular cosmic configuration. Each natal pattern may be compared to a group of terminals in a computer system. Access to information is by means of codes in which certain codes allow greater access than others. Without energy, such as electricity, the computer system cannot function. Without the correct code, the system is inaccessible through lack of a connection, in spite of available energy. Thus the essence of the natal pattern lies in the arrangement of its energy. It is like a key which unlocks and releases energy influences that have an effect on Earth. This unique arrangement of cosmic energy terminals may be considered as an essential energy unit.

CONCEPT: The natal pattern is a vital cosmic code.

Imprint

Cosmic energy imprints each individual at birth to form the natal pattern.

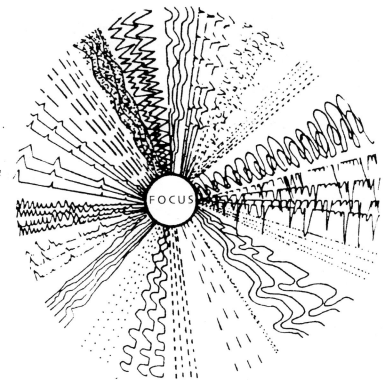

Cosmic Code

The natal pattern is a code in the form of an energy shape programmed to recognize and be recognized by cosmic energy.

Imprinting Concept

These symbolic illustrations show energy focus and imprint (pattern establishment).

Antennae

Each natal pattern is like a center from which antennae radiate at specific degrees, similar to the spokes from the hub in a wheel.[1]

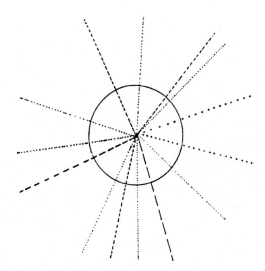

---

1. See "Clock Face: Wheel Analogy" on page 36.

Response

The natal pattern responds to cosmic energy influences according to its imprint.

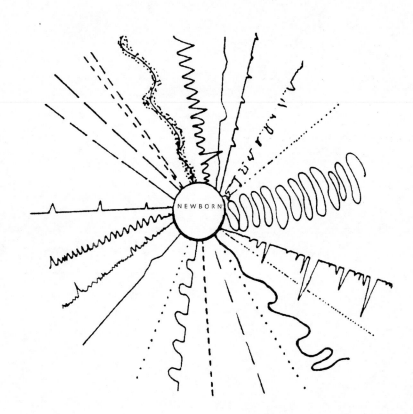

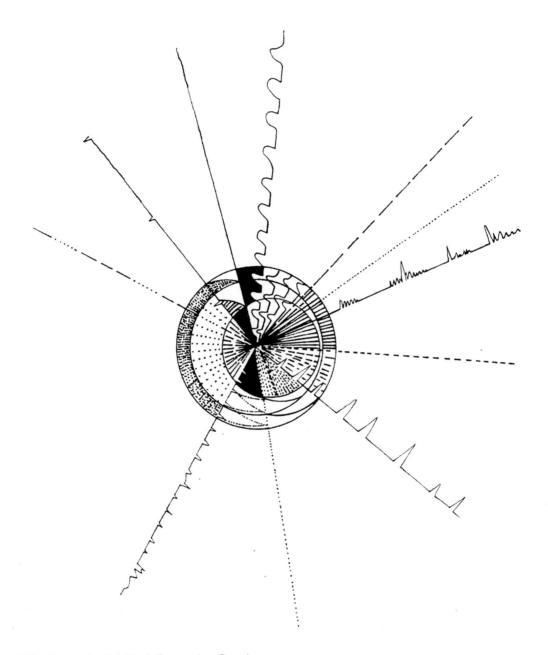

The Natal Pattern Is A Vital Cosmic Code

This shows a natal pattern with a few antennae. Cosmic energy is focused to the center, like the hub of a wheel or the nucleus of a cell. Within the pattern the arrangement of cosmic emissions at the time of birth is captured to form a unique vibration. This vibration responds to cosmic energy influences according to its imprint.

Incoming Energy

INCOMING ENERGY

NATAL
PATTERN OR
COSMIC ENERGY
FOCUS POINT

The Natal Pattern Is A Cosmic Energy Receptor

The symbolic illustration shows a natal pattern as a focus point.

Sensitive Points

Each natal pattern has a unique link with the cosmos according to sensitive points.

In circular concept the natal pattern may be represented on paper as an accurate astrological, or natal chart. The chart, like a cosmic map, is calculated to show the positions of cosmic bodies relative to the Earth at a particular reference point in time. The 'circle' associated with each person, or thing, shows the arrangement of cosmic bodies at the time of birth. In astrological terms, the positions of cosmic bodies in natal charts are known as natal positions. They are important because each position remains sensitive to cosmic emissions and is always influenced by the specific energy principle of the departing cosmic body. In this book, natal positions are termed sensitive points.

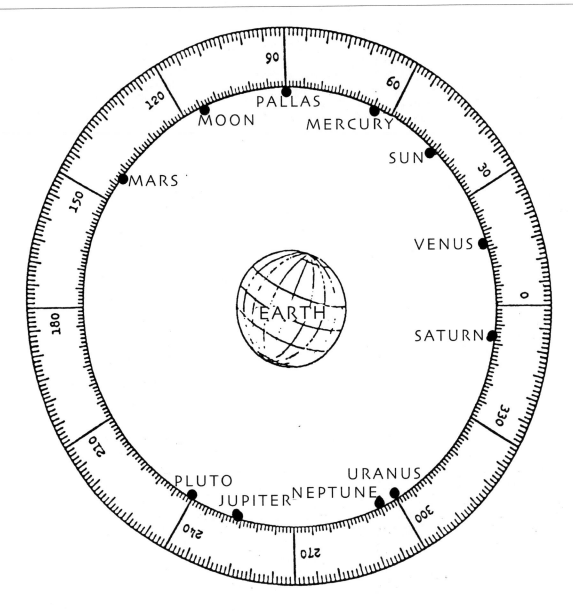

Natal Positions

This shows the positions of a few cosmic bodies on 6th May 1995 (to nearest degree). These degrees become natal positions for births on that day. A natal position retains the influence of the departing cosmic body. All natal positions remain sensitive to cosmic emissions.

From the moment of every birth, each cosmic body begins to move into a different position relative to each natal position. These positions create what is termed the progressed pattern. At any time after birth, a progressed pattern exists which remains in a relationship with the natal pattern.

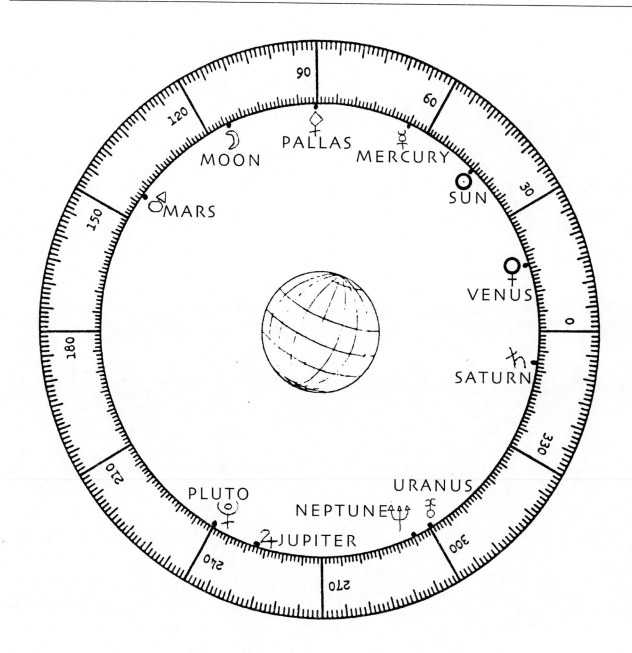

Sensitive Points

Each sensitive point is a cosmic energy terminal.
It is always influenced by the natal energy principle.

Uniqueness

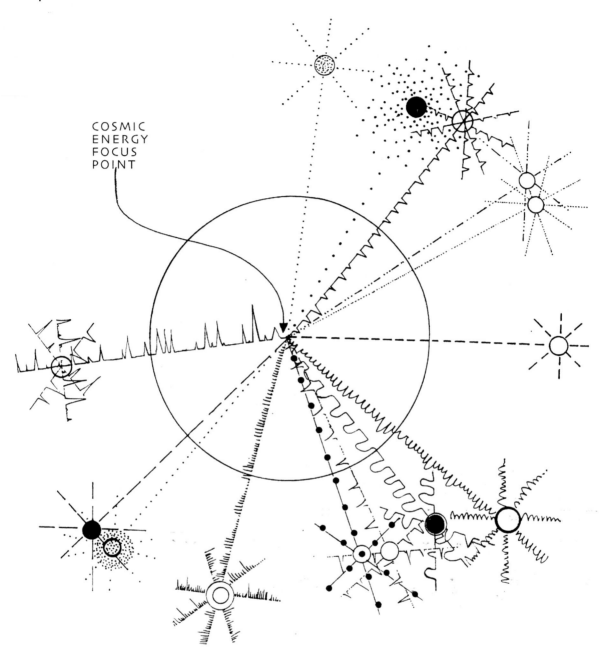

COSMIC
ENERGY
FOCUS
POINT

Imprinting Concept

Each cosmic body emits a specific energy influence.

cf. newborn patterns.

Each natal pattern represents a unique energy arrangement.

Energy principles are affected by cosmic body arrangement, causing positions within a natal pattern to be very important. Within each natal pattern there are always some sensitive points which are linked so that their influence is modified through angular association.

Since all the cosmic bodies are represented in every natal pattern, the configuration determines which principles predominate and the overall nature of the natal influences. In effect, each natal pattern is a unique combination of energy principles. Each resonates at its own frequency and exerts its own influence. Each responds differently to incoming cosmic energy and is, therefore, responsible for its energy expression.

CONCEPT: Cosmic uniqueness determines individuality.

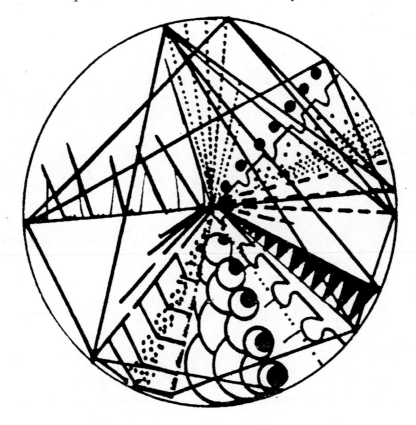

Uniqueness

Different combinations of energy emissions create different patterns.
Different patterns permit uniqueness. Particular patterns give rise to particular people.[4]

---

4. See "Imprinting Concept" on page 11.

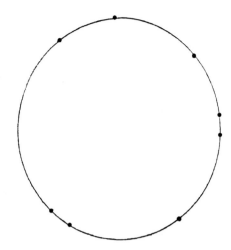

Sensitive Points

Natal pattern association with circle showing sensitive points.

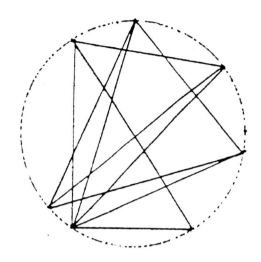

Internal Energy Directions

Natal pattern links among sensitive points are internal energy directions.

External Energy Directions

Sensitive Point Links With The Cosmos Are External Energy Directions

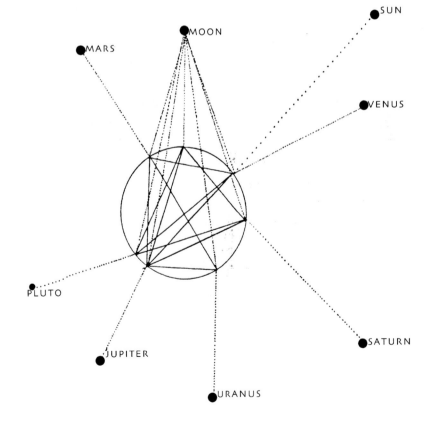

Crystalline Concept

All things exist in cosmic energy shapes.

A natal pattern is the shape of its internal energy links among sensitive points. This spatial arrangement is a geometrical shape, similar to a crystal.[5] Within each pattern these internal links are like energy axes. At all times, as the Earth turns, this shape associates with the prevailing cosmic configuration forming external energy directions or cosmic links, as different cosmic bodies align with different sensitive points. These cosmic links create constantly changing geometrical structures of cosmic body emissions, so that the nature of existence may be likened to a crystalline framework in which each natal pattern is like a moving crystal surrounded by its own unique energy field. In this way all things exist in a cosmic energy shape. These energy shapes do not necessarily conform to the sizes and shapes in the physical world. This may be observed in compatibility, which depends on how the energy shapes fit together.

Cosmic energy activates each pattern during connection, but does not change it. In analogy, the pattern behaves like a crystal in light—it glitters and sparkles, but remains unchanged itself. As moving crystals turn their facets to each other at different angles, natal patterns turn their shapes to one another according to their code.

Natal patterns are also like crystals in the context that they cause energy to flow in a particular way.[6] Sensitive points are terminals through which cosmic energy flows as it links patterns together. Pattern interconnection creates shapes which are essentially crystalline structures. Cosmic body movement, particularly the moon because it is the fastest moving body, causes external energy directions to change quickly as different alignments occur. When alignments change, the external energy shape breaks apart which allows different shapes to come into existence.

It is well to remember that both crystals and individuals are energy arrangements— natal patterns which link with the cosmos. Energy flows among natal patterns according to sensitive point connection. People connect with crystals in the same way that people connect with each other.[7] Natal patterns always identify with a specific shape.[8]

Compatibility in the physical world depends on how these energy shapes fit together.

CONCEPT: All things exist in a crystalline energy field.

---

5. See "Cosmic Energy," p. 2, 4.
6. See "Destiny is an energy direction." on page 184.
7. See "Crystal Analogy" on page 162.
8. See "MV BRAER" on p. 72, and "Uniqueness" on page 18.

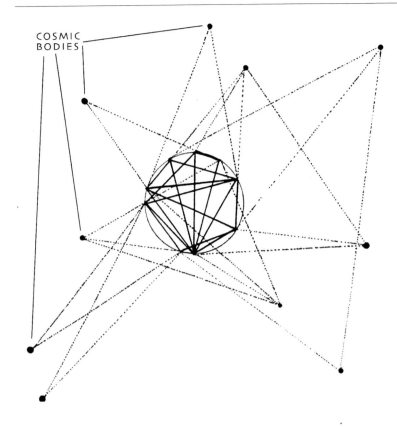

COSMIC
BODIES

Crystalline Concept

Natal pattern within energy field: each natal pattern exists in a constantly changing crystalline shape formed by energy pathways. Natal patterns control this geometric structure which is determined by cosmic body emissions to sensitive points.

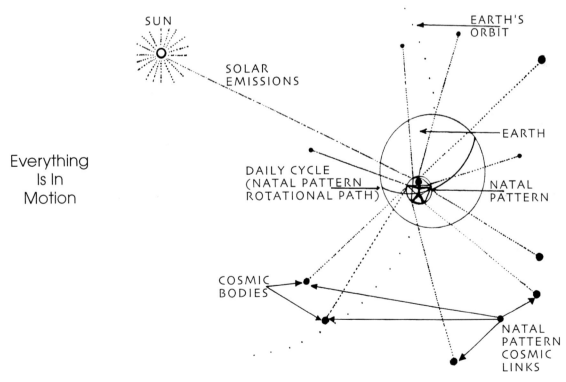

Everything
Is In
Motion

SUN

EARTH'S
ORBIT

SOLAR
EMISSIONS

EARTH

DAILY CYCLE
(NATAL PATTERN
ROTATIONAL PATH)

NATAL
PATTERN

COSMIC
BODIES

NATAL
PATTERN
COSMIC
LINKS

Circular Association

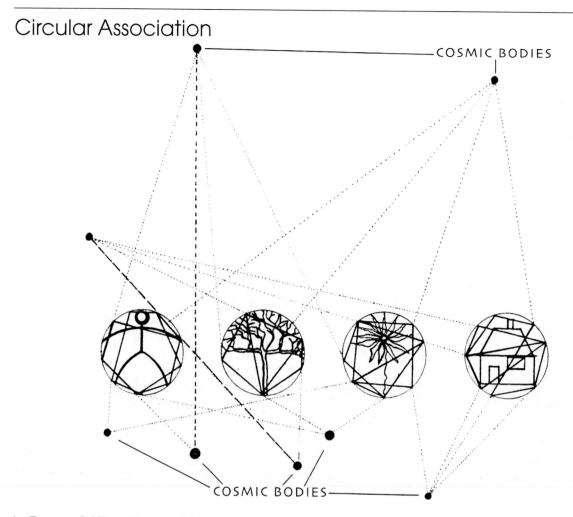

COSMIC BODIES

COSMIC BODIES

In Terms Of The Plane Of The Earth's Orbit, Which Is Like A Huge Disc, Everything On Earth Is Associated With A Circle

The illustration shows internal and external energy directions; the concept of crystalline or geometric shapes; the association with a circle through sensitive points in the natal pattern; and the structural way in which everything is linked. This group of four natal patterns indicates the links between the individual and his environment. For diagrammatic purposes they are drawn separately. In reality they are superimposed and involve complex moving shapes.

A natal pattern is like a birthright belonging exclusively to the individual. It behaves like a protective energy crystal which offers a refuge. In this context everything is both restricted and protected by cosmic energy.

The pattern is the limit of the individual.[9]

---

9. See "Crystalline Concept" on page 20; "All Things Exist In A Cosmic Energy Shape" on page 4; and "An Imprint or Memory Remains" on page 128.

Three • Connection

Cosmic Links

Human connections are not by chance encounter.
A city may boast a million people…yet one meets only a few.
Those who touch one's life represent cosmic energy links.

Connection is a cosmic energy process; it is determined by patterns.

When we arrange to meet someone, it has much less to do with 3:00 PM in our schedule than with our astrological links. We may make appointments ad infinitum, but only the cosmos will allow us to keep them.

Connection is based on cosmic configuration: the configuration of the natal pattern and the way that natal pattern links with the prevailing configuration of the cosmos. This concept is fundamental to the full comprehension of cosmic energy.

Cosmic energy links determine our connections in daily life:
> A boyfriend and girlfriend.
> The owner of a car and the car.
> The owner of the car and the mechanic who maintains it.
> The mechanic and the car.
> A butterfly to wildflowers.
> A tree in the forest to other trees.
> A forest to a hillside.

Cosmic Orchestra

Connections are determined by arrangement (energy patterns) and synchronicity (energy cycles). Each natal pattern has a unique link with the cosmos according to its sensitive points. Each cosmic body orbit is an energy cycle which has a specific influence throughout its duration. Both simple and complex energy cycles are periods of influence and represent cosmic energy pulses. The duration of each pulse is a cyclical interval.

In simple analogy, the cosmos may be compared to a vast orchestra in which each cosmic body is like a different musical instrument. Each body is associated with specific energy emissions as each instrument has its own particular sound, so that cosmic bodies contribute to the different energy influences as the many musical notes contribute to the sound of the orchestra. Cyclical intervals (cosmic body orbits), like musical intervals, determine the various rhythms.

Cyclical intervals prevent everything from happening at once.[1]

CONCEPT: All connections are cosmic energy connections.

Sensitive Points

Natal patterns connect through sensitive points.

The circle, representing the 360 degrees of the zodiac, is the basis for the visual ease in understanding how we connect with each other through our sensitive points. It symbolizes the cyclical nature of all things and the very essence of existence.

From the moment of birth, as cosmic bodies move away from their original positions in any natal pattern, the vacant positions remain sensitive to the departing cosmic energy sources. These sensitive points are terminals for cosmic energy—contact points through which energy may flow from the cosmos to Earth. They may be determined mathematically. Sensitive points are permanent links with the cosmos and, therefore, very important positions in natal patterns. Common and related sensitive points among natal patterns allow pattern interconnection on Earth. The more sensitive points involved, the greater the opportunity for connection. The greater the number of common degrees, the more involvement of one pattern with another. The more cosmic bodies at any one degree, the greater the complexity of energy expression during connection.

The cosmos is the frame of reference for all comparison on Earth.

Patterns connect because they have sensitive points in common.

Pattern interactions are influenced by specific combinations of energy principles.

Once this concept of connection is acknowledged, it allows the individual to identify with the universe—to understand that everything is linked by cosmic energy and to realize the significance of all things. In this acceptance one begins to comprehend the deeper meaning of existence.

CONCEPT: All connections occur through sensitive points.

---

1. See "Cyclical Interval" on page 76.

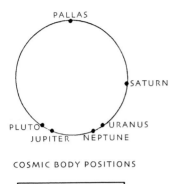

COSMIC BODY POSITIONS

ENERGY SOURCES
IN THE COSMOS

SENSITIVE POINTS

ENERGY TERMINALS
ON EARTH

The Natal Influence Remains Like An Unseen Presence

At the time of birth, energy sources in the cosmos (cosmic body positions) become energy terminals on Earth (natal positions, or sensitive points in a natal pattern on Earth).

Each natal pattern connects with the cosmos according to its code. Pattern interconnection depends on sensitive points at common or related degrees

Common Degrees

This diagram shows two different natal patterns, each illustrating eight sensitive points and four common degrees as shared energy focus points.

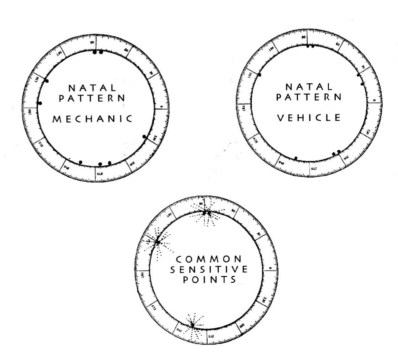

NATAL
PATTERN

MECHANIC

NATAL
PATTERN

VEHICLE

COMMON
SENSITIVE
POINTS

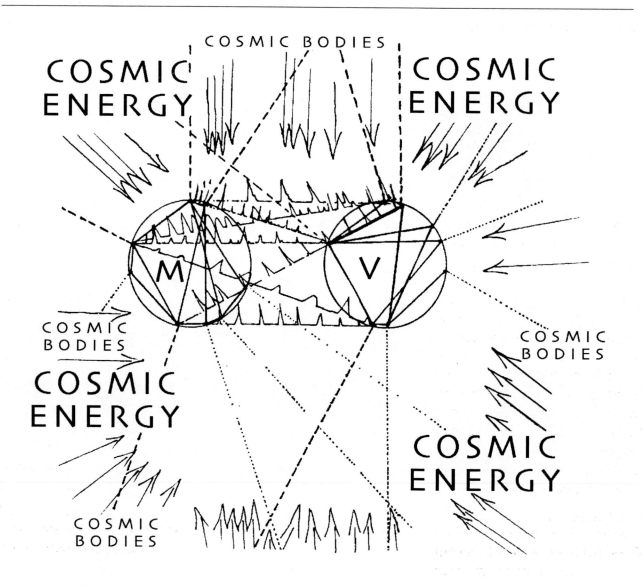

All Connections Are Cosmic Energy Connections

    M natal pattern mechanic.
    V natal pattern vehicle.
    ....permanent sensitive point links with cosmos.
    ----activated sensitive point links with cosmic body
    ^^^interaction links among sensitive points during mechanic and vehicle connection.

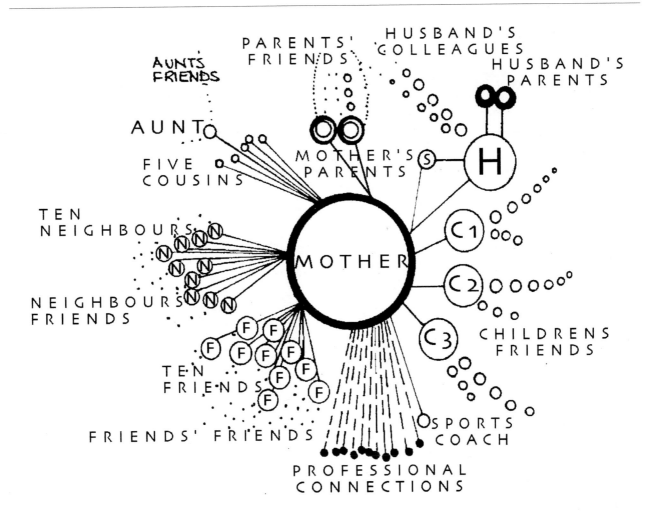

Human Linking

C1 C2 C3 children
H husband
S husband's sister
F friends
N neighbors

In this diagram every circle or dot represents a human natal pattern in a group where the mother's pattern is the main, or common, linking pattern. The mother is closely connected to her husband, children, the grand-parents, an aunt, five cousins, the husband's sister, friends, neighbors, and a sports coach. The professional group includes doctors, teachers, librarians, hairdressers, etc. All others are extensions of her circle through intermittent contact. In cosmic terms, the mother is neither more nor less important than the others, but within her own realm she feels herself at the center. In the same way each of us is the centre of our own universe, it is therefore easy to forget that everyone else is part of the system and is to be considered in the mosaic of cosmic energy. Within this context everyone is linked to everyone else, no one is missing in the cosmic jigsaw puzzle.

Picture of Energy: Sequence

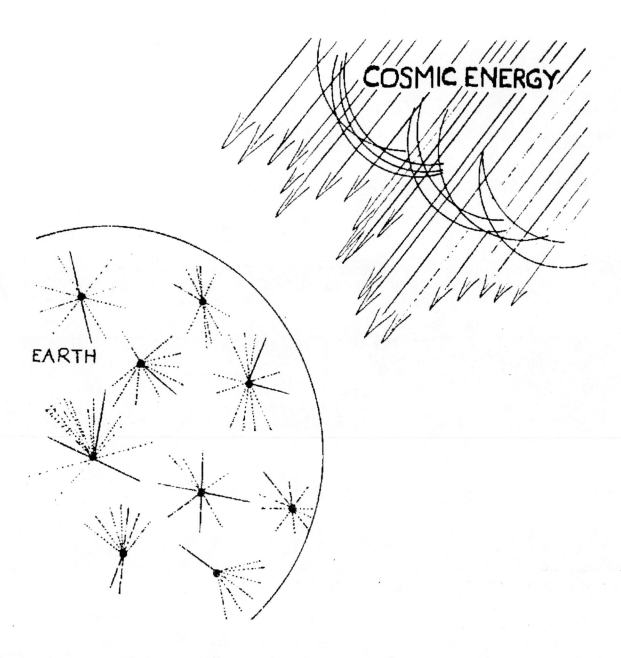

Natal Patterns Are Cosmic Energy Terminals On Earth[2]

This symbolic illustration shows cosmic energy flowing to Earth and focus points for this energy in the form of natal patterns (depicted as dots with antennae) of varying sensitivity to each cosmic body.

2. See "The Natal Influence Remains Like An Unseen Presence" on page 25.

Picture of Energy

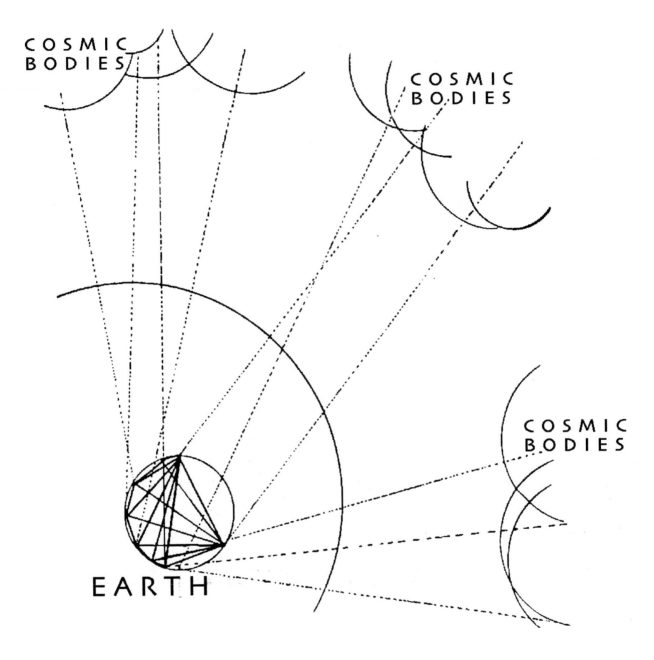

Sensitive Points Direct Energy Flow For Each Pattern

This symbolic illustration shows a natal pattern as an energy focus point and incoming cosmic energy connecting with the pattern through sensitive points. This diagram expands an energy focus point (depicted as a dot in the previous diagram) to reveal the geometric nature of the natal pattern.

Energy Sequence

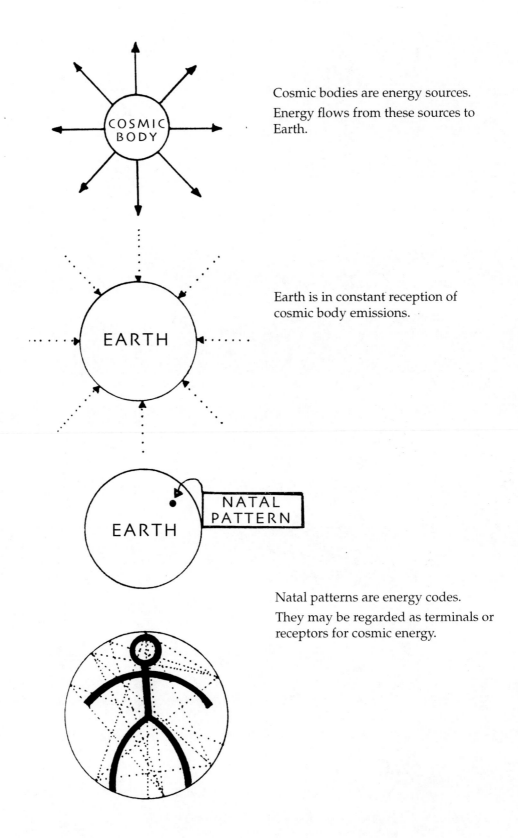

Cosmic bodies are energy sources. Energy flows from these sources to Earth.

Earth is in constant reception of cosmic body emissions.

Natal patterns are energy codes. They may be regarded as terminals or receptors for cosmic energy.

Energy Sequence

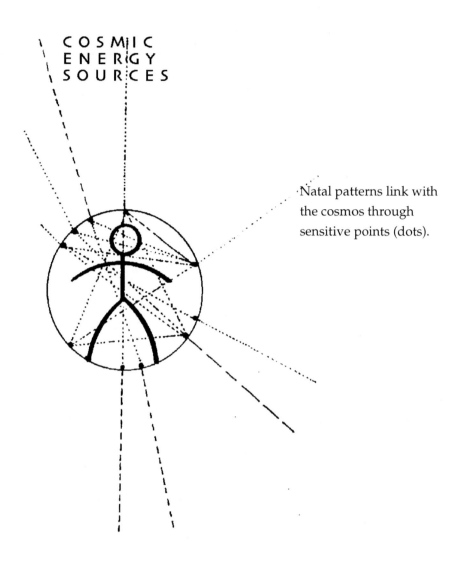

COSMIC
ENERGY
SOURCES

·Natal patterns link with the cosmos through sensitive points (dots).

Circuitry

Links with the cosmos are energy pathways. They form during alignments.

Cosmic links permit particular emissions to influence particular positions on Earth, and therefore, particular degrees in natal patterns. These degrees correspond to particular sensitive points.

Cosmic links initiate natal pattern interaction on Earth.

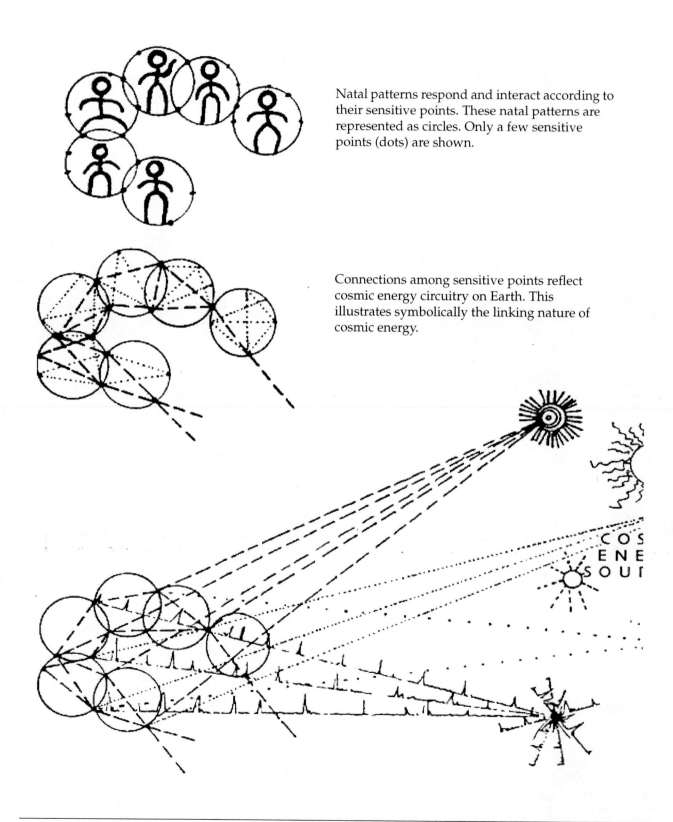

Natal patterns respond and interact according to their sensitive points. These natal patterns are represented as circles. Only a few sensitive points (dots) are shown.

Connections among sensitive points reflect cosmic energy circuitry on Earth. This illustrates symbolically the linking nature of cosmic energy.

Energy Directions

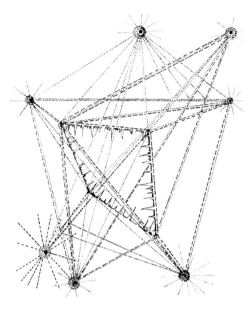

Angular Network

The illustration shows four natal patterns (dots) linked to the cosmos and each other.

The cosmic grid is an angular network of energy directions. Cosmos-Earth connections are like energy pathways, or access routes. Each link is an energy direction. Interconnecting energy directions form an angular network like a labyrinth of defined spaces—momentary shapes in space. This vast network of alignments among sensitive points forms the cosmic energy grid. It is like a connective tissue for it links all things together. As the Earth spins in space, cosmic energy sweeps through the natal pattern of all things. Alignments form and change. Cosmic energy rearranges itself. New things come into being in the continuum.

Interaction

Cosmic energy derives its power from its linking capacity.

Without connective links, cosmic energy is isolated. Nothing happens. There is no event. Time and space are undefined. Simple in principle, yet complex in effect, the way in which everything connects is determined by cosmic energy arrangement.

The interaction of natal patterns is made possible by the movement of cosmic bodies and is the means by which cosmic energy manifests on Earth. In whatever way natal patterns connect with the cosmos (individual expression) and with one another (natal pattern interaction) is the way in which cosmic energy will express itself. Individual expression occurs because each natal pattern has a unique link with the cosmos. It is observed in characteristics, personality traits, and individual behavior, which explains why one person is morose and another exhibits a happy disposition. Natal pattern interaction is responsible for everything which happens—serious encounters, light-hearted moments, dangerous situations.

Natal patterns and the interaction of these patterns account for and explain affinity: the reason why one is drawn to certain people or certain things; why one person must have an aquamarine and why another insists on a certain moonstone. It is why some people are cat lovers, and why wonderful bonds exist between humans and their pets. The special feeling is a cosmic energy link, which becomes evident when the natal patterns are compared.

Cosmic Discrimination

Cosmic energy recognizes the pattern.

The natal pattern is like an invisible energy shape with antennae at sensitive points which scan the immediate sphere of the individual. As contact from the cosmos occurs, particular antennae respond by strengthening connective links until perfect alignment. Thus, the natal pattern not only provides the antennae which connect the individual to the cosmos, but also controls the response through these links. In this way the cosmos controls the individual through the natal pattern.

In everyday life cosmic discrimination is observed when only one individual breaks a leg while mountaineering. It is explained in terms of the natal pattern response to a prevailing cosmic arrangement which triggers a specific interaction within a particular individual. No one else is affected in the same way because each natal pattern is unique and responds differently.[3]

The natal pattern link with the cosmos determines energy expression. This means that responses to cosmic body movement and the energy principles involved determine the effect of cosmic influences. The process is continuous. It is always in a forward thrust, which determines energy direction—individual energy paths, or destiny—within the system.[4]

Clock Face Analogy

An old-fashioned clock face shows the hours, minutes, and seconds of the day by means of three hands which point toward the circumference of a calibrated circle. An astrological chart may be likened to a much more complex clock face around which the cosmic bodies orbit at various speeds, or their respective cyclical intervals. A natal chart (the representation of a natal pattern in two dimensions) is analogous to a personal clock face that is unique to the individual. As cosmic bodies move in their orbits, the prevailing cosmic pattern continually superimposes itself on each individual clock face. When links between cosmic bodies and sensitive points form, the energy directions may also be likened to the hands of a vast cosmic clock. Response occurs as these cosmos-Earth connections are made. Due to natal pattern uniqueness, there is a different energy response within each individual (termed energy expression) as exposure to these influences occurs. Connection and interaction at sensitive points determine events in the life of each individual. When particular connections occur, profound events happen for each individual, until one specific cosmic superimposition results in death.

---

3. See MV BRAER, p. 72.
4. See "Future Thrust" on page 51.

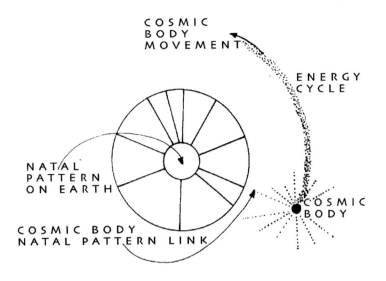

A Natal Pattern Is Like A Personal Clock Face

The illustration shows a natal pattern in terms of sensitive points (dots) around a circle, like a personal clock face. The diagram is expanded to show that cosmic links are like irregular spokes of a wheel. These links may be likened to the hands of a clock. Cosmic links occur as cosmic bodies move. The arrow points in the direction of cosmic body movement. Each body moves according to its cyclical interval.

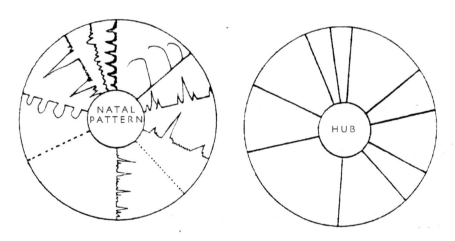

The Natal Pattern is the Pre-Cursor of What Happens on Earth

Imagine a natal pattern as the hub of a wheel from which irregular spokes radiate at various angles. The spokes may be likened to antennae from the natal positions of cosmic bodies (sensitive points in the natal pattern). Each antenna represents a permanent energy link with the cosmos. Consider the Earth as the hub of another wheel (a geocentric wheel) in which cosmic bodies (energy sources) are positioned around the circumference or rim of the wheel. As a natal pattern (hub) rotates with the Earth and gradually moves around the sun, the antennae align with different cosmic bodies as they move around the rim of the geocentric wheel. Alignments through antennae (spokes) to sensitive points allow cosmic energy to flow to the hub of the wheel (natal pattern). The response of a natal pattern to the cosmos through these energy links determines how cosmic energy will express itself or manifest on Earth. Interconnection among natal patterns, referred to as energy pattern relationships, determines events on Earth.

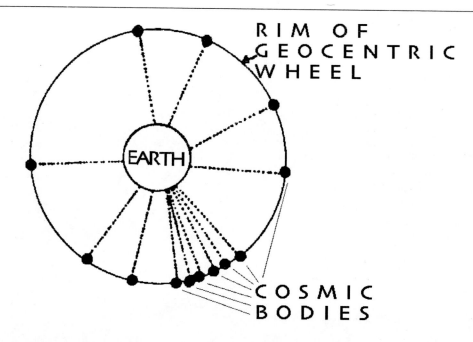

Clock Face: Wheel Analogy

The two wheels may be imagined as two separately moving discs within a constantly changing energy environment in which the interaction between Earth and the cosmos occurs through juxtaposition.

Synchronicity

Connection is linked with energy cycles.

Not only are people linked with each other in particular ways, connections are synchronized by energy cycles.[5]

As the Earth rotates, each natal pattern experiences a daily cycle in which prevailing positions of cosmic bodies align with sensitive points in each natal pattern. Linked energy influences combine principles which determine how cosmic energy will express itself.

Within the vastness of cosmic momentum, different natal patterns continually meet and interact through cycle synchronicity. Each encounter is an energy focus point in space, known as the merge point position or encounter point.

---

5. See "Cosmic Orchestra" on page 23.

Encounter Point

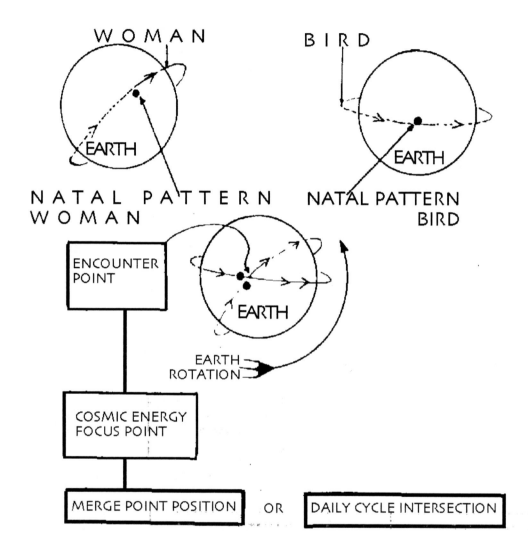

DAILY CYCLE
(MOVEMENT WITH THE EARTH)

Natal Pattern Connection Occurs at the Merge Point Position: The Cyclical Intersection Which is Brought About by Cycle Synchronicity

Everything moves with the Earth in a daily cycle. However, each natal pattern path, or individual cycle, is different because it depends on cycle synchronicity. Natal pattern connections are cosmic energy encounters. They occur at merge point positions or cosmic energy focus points during daily cycle intersections. In this illustration the paths are widely separated for diagrammatic purposes. Thus the huge bird which soared on a thermal current towards the woman seemed to have appeared out of nowhere. In reality, the bird was approaching the woman before entering her field of vision.[6]

---

6. See "Cycles of the Day" on page 91; and "Concept: Connection is in an energy focus point." on page 40.

Synchronicity

Cosmic energy cycles bring people and events together…and force them apart.
Thus separation is as much a part of cosmic energy expression as connection.

Divorce and marriage are polarities in the universal order of things. They are opposite energy expressions involving the union between two people, and are of equal importance. Like birth or death, neither is to be judged in terms of good or bad.

If natal patterns do not have a connecting factor, they will not, and cannot meet. In this way, the natal pattern is a controlling factor in the cosmos and of profound significance. It may be considered as an essential energy unit for it is ultimately responsible for how things happen on Earth.

The relationship of one energy pattern to another is the underlying principle of connection, for it determines how cosmic energy will express itself through the synchronicity of cosmic bodies and sensitive points. Human relationships are cosmic energy relationships. It is how we all fit in, and illustrates cosmic control through energy cycles which determine when people and things appear and disappear in our lives.

Thus the complexity of existence, which includes the life cycle, is due to energy pattern relationships: the configuration of energy connection rather than the energy itself. This emphasizes the importance of the pattern, the arrangement of the different principles which interact and cause all things to be the way they are.

CONCEPT: All relationships are cosmic energy relationships.

Four • Focus

Position

The cosmos is the frame of reference for all things on Earth.

Pilots use satellite geometry to identify exact positions on Earth. This is possible because each man-made satellite emits a special signal. In the same way that signals from satellites pinpoint positions for pilots in flight, emissions from cosmic bodies pinpoint particular positions on Earth through the geometry of cosmic body alignments. The positions where cosmic body emissions converge are merge point positions or cosmic energy focus points.

All things on Earth are in a position relative to everything else, so that everything hinges on position: sensitive point positions in natal patterns, cosmic body positions in cosmic configurations and positions of converging alignments, or energy focus points on Earth. As cosmic body movement brings energy emissions into focus, positions on Earth become focus points for these emissions through cycle synchronicity. Wherever cosmic energy connects with the Earth becomes a focus point for natal pattern interaction.

Sensitive points correspond to particular degrees in the circle of the Earth's orbital path at the moment of birth. When alignments from cosmic bodies to the Earth coincide with sensitive point positions, those degrees become focus points for natal pattern interaction. Natal influences (energy principles) at the degree of alignment are emphasized. In this way alignments determine natal pattern connection with the cosmos and interconnection among the patterns. This process explains why different things happen at different times, in different places, and to different people in a continuum of moments on Earth.

Sensitive points in natal patterns are terminals for incoming cosmic energy. Every twenty-four hours, as the Earth rotates, each sensitive point in each natal pattern is exposed to the prevailing cosmic configuration. Response to this bombardment of cosmic body emissions occurs during alignments to these points and happens at the focus point position on Earth.

A tree beside the path continually accepts the prevailing cosmic influences in a single location. When the moment occurs, it cannot avoid the woodcutter's axe. Thus, its lifelong position becomes the death site for the tree, killed not by lightning, disease, or old age, but in a sudden violent act. The mobile individual may seem to be less helpless and avoid situations by running away. It is not so. Whether the individual walks along a country path or remains in one place like a tree, the natal pattern always determines the response to incoming cosmic energy.

Death comes to the individual as it comes to a tree and to all things—in a focus point position where the energy expression in the moment manifests as death.[1]

CONCEPT: Connection is in an energy focus point.

Position

Although cosmic energy is everywhere, it needs to be focused. It gains potential through a collection process in which cosmic body emissions exert full force during perfect alignment. As energy gathers towards a focus point, the approaching alignment increases the cosmic body influence. As cosmic connection occurs energy shapes define natal pattern interaction. The shapes which form are defined by prevailing alignments to natal pattern energy structures. Thus, shape is an integral part of cosmic energy processes. For this reason cosmic energy needs space in which to express itself. This means that natal patterns are always surrounded by energy shapes which jostle, or compete, for space as connections are made. In the contest some shapes cannot form as they should, causing energy misfit. Humans experience uncomfortable feelings, unfinished or hurried conversations, snatched phrases in passing, often leading to withdrawal. It is particularly evident in Saturn connections.[2]

When a position on Earth is occupied by many natal patterns (house pattern, room pattern, human patterns), interconnection among all patterns fills the space with energy in a particular way and creates a feeling of crowding. Overcrowding causes stress for this reason. Tensions build until released by energy rearrangement. In human terms it may mean moving to a larger building, or departure of some people. It is known as making room. In cosmic terms it is fewer patterns well arranged in the available space. Conversely, when natal patterns are perfectly connected there is very little stress. They can be in close proximity and not feel crowded because they fit well together. It is most common in compatible relationships.

Focus Points

Cosmic energy exerts its influence through changing energy focus points.

The code which determines the natal pattern remains constant.[3] It is the configuration of the cosmos which constantly changes. As energy sources move relative to everything else, everything experiences a change in energy influence due to changing energy fields.

Humans need to remember that we are not energy sources. We are, like all things on Earth, energy terminals that respond to energy sources in the form of forces on Earth. How

---

1. See "The MV BRAER" on page 72; "Inevitability" on page 52; and "Perspective" on page 182.
2. See "Portrait of Saturn" on page 61.
3. See "Crystalline Concept" on page 20.

we respond is determined by our natal pattern, the unique code for each individual. In this context we may regard ourselves as energy receptors.

Shape

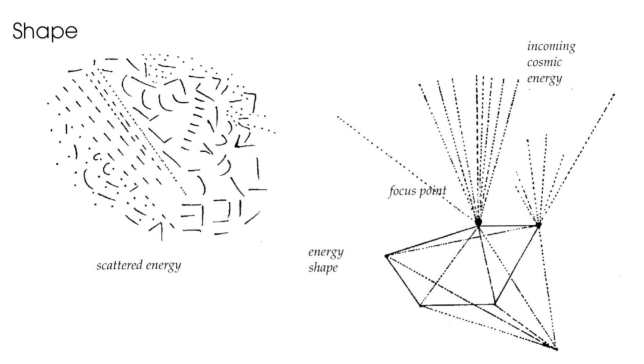

scattered energy

energy shape

incoming cosmic energy

focus point

Cosmic Energy Involves Shape

Cosmic energy gains potential as it gathers towards a point. The illustration shows unfocused, or scattered energy, and focused energy, which gathers towards sensitive points forming a shape as connections are made. It is a process of:

focus	point of converging energy
connection	cosmic link
gathering	energy influence building prior to perfect alignment
interaction	energy expression in the moment
shape formation	energy definition
dimension creation	energy imprint, cosmic memory

CONCEPT: Shape is an integral part of cosmic energy processes.[4]

---

4. See "Shape Definition" on page 114 ; and page 1.

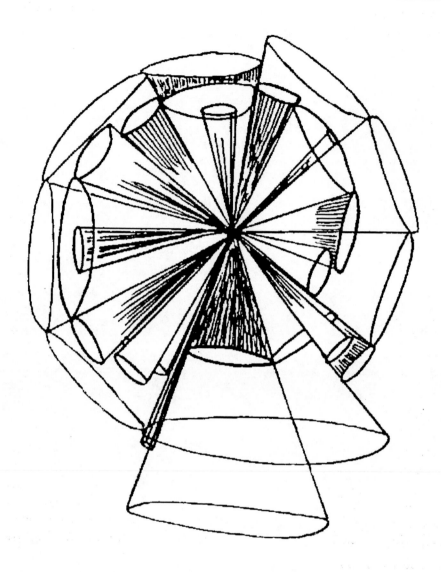

The Natal Pattern is a Center To Which Cosmic Emissions Are Focused

At all times this energy focus point is surrounded by incoming cosmic energy which forms cones that disintegrate as alignments to sensitive points change.

Although the visible shape of the human body seems to be the same from day to day, the surrounding energy shape in which we live (human aura) changes constantly because it responds to alignments which change as cosmic bodies move. When our response to the cosmos makes us feel expansive, we experience difficulty when there is insufficient space for expansion to occur or when the space is filled with other shapes incompatible with the space we need. It is like wanting a large, clean surface on which to lay out fabric only to find the room is filled with rusting old engines like a neglected garage.

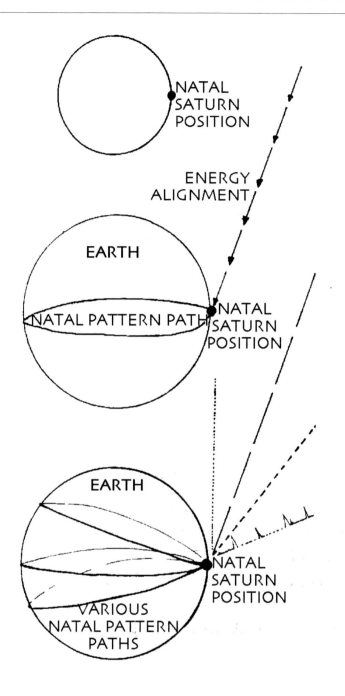

Natal patterns are energy focus points and occupy specific positions on Earth. The natal Saturn position equates to a focus point space.

The natal pattern movement on Earth is a spiral around the sun.

Cosmic energy movement on Earth is a circuit among natal patterns that interlink through sensitive points. This figure shows various natal Saturn positions. Much cosmic energy has passed through this point over many millions of years. During the present lifetime of the individual, all cosmic emissions that pass through this position are always influenced by Saturn. Different positions on Earth allow different lifestyles, therefore Earth positions are extremely important.

For diagrammatic purposes these three figures are shown separately. In reality they are one—the natal Saturn position within the 360 degrees of the zodiac.

Activity on Earth is directly related to movement in the cosmos. This activity, or energy expression, is essentially cyclical because cosmic body movement is cyclical.

Five • Expression

Momentary Nature

Nothing happens by chance.

Everything which happens is a passing expression of cosmic energy: the life cycle of a tree, a smile on a face, a fatal car crash. There are no mistakes, no accidents, only changes which allow new things to come into being—the people we meet, the things we do, the possessions we acquire. Everything is related to a cosmic influence and determined by a response to incoming cosmic energy. Since everything which happens occurs through energy pattern relationships, energy expression is dependent on the connection and interaction of natal patterns. It is momentary, for it corresponds to a continually changing arrangement of energy alignments.

This cosmic Earth interaction is responsible for human and animal behavior, global and individual events, geophysical rearrangement.

Shape

Energy expression defines shapes in space.

A physicist defines energy as anything capable of producing a force, and a force as a push or pull in a given direction. In vector diagrams forces are represented by lines. A number of forces acting on an object will therefore outline a specific shape.

Cosmic links are forces and may also be represented by lines in diagrams. In reality cosmic links are energy pathways from bodies in the cosmos (energy sources) to the sensitive points in natal patterns through focus points on Earth.

These links outline shapes in space. Since infinite numbers of sensitive points are involved, numerous shapes come into existence as different alignments occur. These shapes are formed in the moment of energy connection and last for the duration of the energy expression. Thus each shape represents a particular moment. Each moment in turn is associated with an event on Earth. In this way, events on Earth are records of cosmic energy expressions, moments which may be identified by specific shapes that may be linked with a cosmic configuration.

In this book these shapes are termed energy structures.

CONCEPT: A moment is a shape in space.

Structural Concept

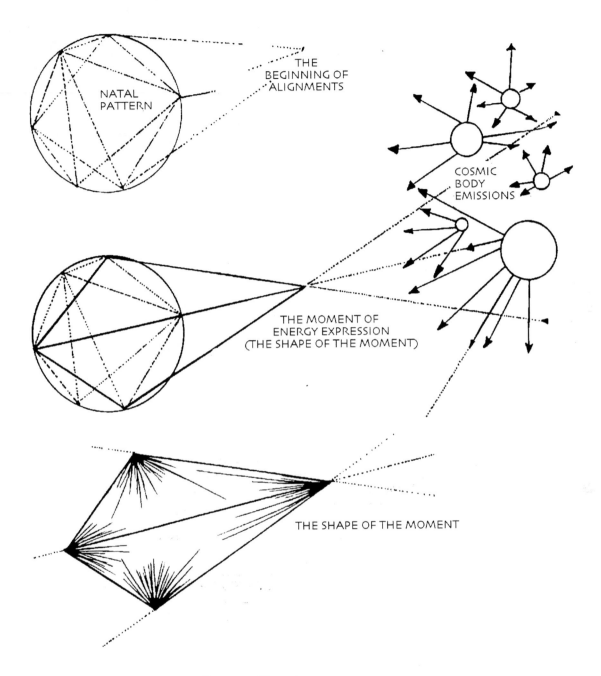

THE
BEGINNING OF
ALIGNMENTS

NATAL
PATTERN

COSMIC
BODY
EMISSIONS

THE MOMENT OF
ENERGY EXPRESSION
(THE SHAPE OF THE MOMENT)

THE SHAPE OF THE MOMENT

Each Moment Captures an Energy Structure

Cosmic energy links create a shape in the moment of energy expression. The shape or energy structure is specific to the moment. It may be likened to a reaction chamber.

Energy Fits the Shape

In the moment of energy expression, there is one shape within which particular patterns, or energy units, connect. The shape contains the forces (energy influences) during the moment and corresponds to the space of occurrence. This diagram is drawn in an artistic way to represent the concept—energy fits the shape.

Structural Concept

All things are associated with moments:
a wedding ceremony;
the rhythm of a city;
the evolution of the forest.

Cosmic energy interactions with natal patterns are all moments. Each moment captures the energy structure which is created in the process, and describes the shape formed by energy directions during expression. As cosmic bodies move, cosmic links change, bringing different energy principles into the arena of influence. Different cosmic links among natal patterns cause constantly changing responses which account for daily activity and events on Earth where each event corresponds to a particular moment in the universe. Only once does cosmic energy express itself in that particular way. Each moment for each individual represents a portion of an individual lifetime. These are the moments of our lives.

Within this perpetual cosmic interplay is the dimension of human existence in physical reality.[1] As cosmic energy continues to rearrange itself, it forms energy sensitive shapes—dimensions known to humans as time.

Geometrical Nature

Cosmic linking is of a geometrical nature; it involves shape through the architecture of alignments. It is how the cosmos exerts subtle forces on Earth.

If it were possible to observe cosmic energy, it would show multidimensional shapes in motion, interlinked in a vast network of incredible intricacy. Simple in principle, yet complex in combination, it would emphasize the importance of structure, and show that the connections among natal patterns matter more than the energy itself because each connection contributes to the form of a different structure. Each energy structure involves different energy principles and has a different effect.

At all times a natal pattern is connected with other dimensions. The human experience is a feeling of familiarity with something: a place, a person, or a knowledge of a subject without study, like a natural talent. At the present time conscious and subconscious

---

1. See "Energy Moves into Space" on page 107; "Minutes/Moments" on page 110; and "Allotted Time" on page 165.

awareness of these things is not always possible through soul memory. For many, if not most, connection with other dimensions is through an outside influence.[2]

Momentary Structure

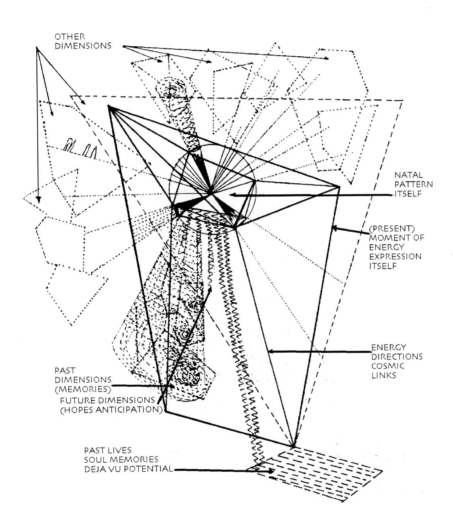

A Moment is a Shape in Space

This shows the moment in angular form which occurs at exact alignment

---

Component Parts: Picture of Energy

The natal pattern itself isolated for diagrammatic purpose.

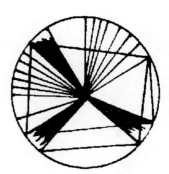

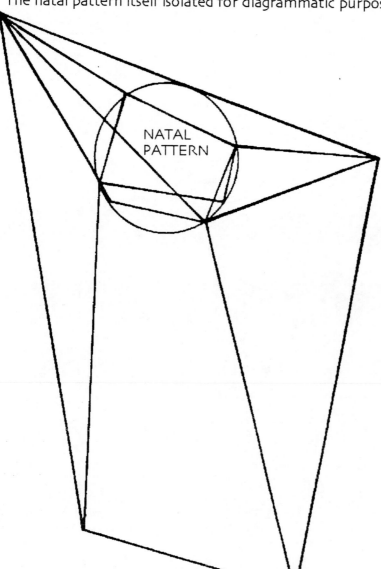

NATAL
PATTERN

A Specific Shape Exists for Each Moment of Expression

This illustration shows the moment of energy expression isolated for diagrammatic purposes. For each moment a specific shape exists because each moment has a different energy structure. For each energy expression which occurs, a dimension is created.

Picture of Energy

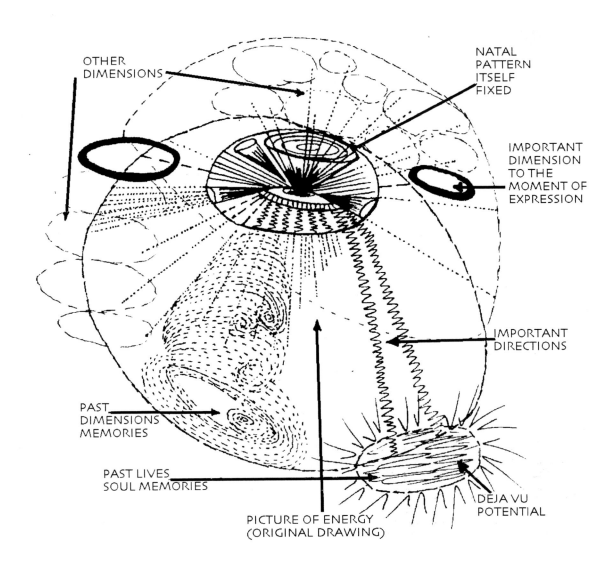

OTHER DIMENSIONS

NATAL PATTERN ITSELF FIXED

IMPORTANT DIMENSION TO THE MOMENT OF EXPRESSION

IMPORTANT DIRECTIONS

PAST DIMENSIONS MEMORIES

PAST LIVES SOUL MEMORIES

PICTURE OF ENERGY (ORIGINAL DRAWING)

DEJA VU POTENTIAL

Structural Concept

This shows the moment stretched or pulled as the cosmos moves, so that the picture of energy exhibits curves before and after exact alignment.[3]

The picture of energy depicts a natal pattern activated by cosmic links within a moment of energy expression. Energy directions pervade the shape of the moment as they connect with other dimensions, including memory, soul memory, "déjà vu," and the potential for future expression. At all times a natal pattern is linked with the soul memory. Access to this memory is like human-memory recall; one cannot always remember, rather like access to a computer in which the circuit is not connecting in a particular way at that time.

---

3. See "Amorphous Form" on page 98.

Picture of Energy

Mosaic in a Time Frame.

This illustrates a section through a moment, a "slice" which appears as a mosaic.

It is impossible to extricate a natal pattern from its moments.
Although separate in essence, they are inextricably linked.

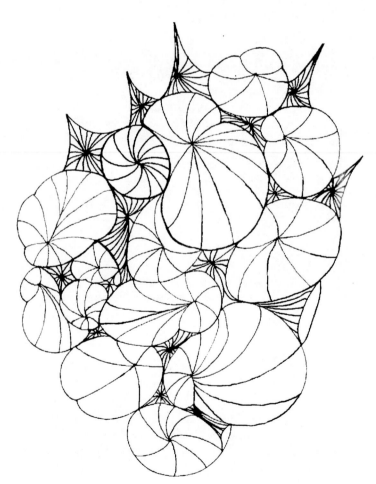

Moments in Rhythm

This symbolic illustration shows the pulse of the universe as a rhythm of moments. Each moment is connected to another in an energy continuum. Each energy expression causes vibrations which contribute to the universal rhythm or "energy grid."

Future Thrust

Cosmic energy cycles determine universal order.

Cosmic energy movement on Earth is defined by moments, or energy structures. Particular structures permit movement in a particular way, like wind through the trees. In a windy area, the wind forces growth that is favorable for survival. The trees become twisted and bent, but their contorted structure permits the wind to pass through freely without breaking the trunks or branches. The shapes of the trees allow them to survive.

A natal pattern is similar to a tree in the wind; its structure determines its life cycle around and through which cosmic energy moves. Evolutionary direction is also influenced in this way.[4]

Cosmic energy expression causes the flow of events. Termed "future thrust," it is an energy direction from the preceding moment (the past), through the present, and into the future. The moments happen in sequence because each moment is formed by different cosmic links. Cosmic energy thus propels itself, or advances into space.

Momentary sequence is similar to a circle of people holding hands. Everyone is linked, yet each individual only touches two other people. As cosmic energy expresses itself and moves into the next shape, it leaves the past, enters the present, and eventually moves into the future. Nothing is possible unless the past has occurred. The present is like someone holding the past and future together, like a parent who links a grandparent with a grandchild.

In the sequence of events, everything happens in order. One thing leads to another; one thing precedes the next—like a chain reaction. A woman must first be a young girl, a youth precedes a man. Every event has its own position in the sequence. Everything has its place and fits into the whole, like the pieces of a vast multi-dimensional jigsaw puzzle in motion. Although the individual may think that what happens is through personal decision, or chance, there is a deeper meaning to the apparently mundane order. All things occur through energy pattern relationships and are part of the greater scheme of things.

The circuit for cosmic energy movement on Earth is a network of connections dictated by natal pattern interaction.[5]

CONCEPT: Momentary sequence is an energy direction.

---

4. See "Crystalline Concept" on page 21.
5. See "Cosmic links initiate natal pattern interaction on Earth." on page 32.

Inevitability

Events on Earth are directly related to cosmic energy.

Everything on Earth takes place through cosmic energy interaction. Energy expression occurs in a sequence of cosmic body alignments to natal positions between birth and death. As each cosmic body aligns with a natal position, that sensitive point is intensified for the individual. The combination of connecting energy principles determines the mode of expression. Thus events on Earth reflect cosmic configurations, for they are always associated with the prevailing cosmic energy arrangement. Consider a car collision. What causes the one which happens and prevents another which does not? Prior to an impending collision, particular natal patterns are moving towards the same position on Earth.[6] As cosmic energy aligns with that space, it connects with common or related degrees in each of those natal patterns. Nothing prevents interaction in the moment which manifests as a collision. Prior to a car collision which does not occur, natal patterns enter a space but are not synchronized; there is no interconnection. The energy structure which forms in that moment does not fit the shape for a car collision.

Cosmic energy principles express in specific ways. When cosmic energy is arranged in a particular way, it must and will express according to that arrangement.

CONCEPT: Inevitability.

---

6. See "Cosmic Discrimination" on page 34; MV BRAER page 72; "Energy Fits the Shape" on page 118; "Concept: Connection is in an energy focus point." on page 40; and "Encounter Point" on page 37.

Six • Effect

Cosmic Configuration

All cosmic bodies have an effect on Earth.

Astrology acknowledges the existence of cosmic body influences by their effect on Earth. The evidence, which has been accumulated over thousands of years, shows that this effect depends entirely on arrangement, in particular, planetary positions in cosmic configurations. Although the energy which emanates from each cosmic body is specific at source, the influence on Earth is modified because emissions are always in association with each other. For this reason the effect of cosmic bodies is mostly observed as a combined influence. These fluctuating combinations contribute an elusive quality to cosmic energy.

Cosmic energy exerts its force at energy focus points. These positions are determined by alignments to sensitive points in natal patterns and maybe likened to electrical outlets in a house. Each time a plug is inserted, energy activates the device in a particular way. Alignments form the cosmic energy grid which links all things together in particular ways. What matters is the linking within and among energy arrangements (configurations in the cosmos and natal patterns on Earth). Connection through linking determines how cosmic body emissions and, therefore, cosmic energy is combined. Emissions from energy sources combine to produce specific influences, or the continually changing forces on Earth. Different forces exert different influences and cause different effects.[1] It should be noted that within each combination of influences, there are also subtle differences in effect due to different angles of alignment.[2] In addition, there is an astrological hierarchy in which cosmic bodies are assigned to and are responsible for specific things, so that within the discipline itself, astrology accounts for all things.[3]

Two brief interpretations are given to illustrate the effect of different combinations of planetary energy.

---

1. With intent to emphasize the specificity of cosmic body influences, the planets are sometimes personified to illustrate their particular energy influences, like different personalities.
2. These are not discussed here. See Suggested Reading, *The Combination of Stellar Influences*, p. 203.
3. See "Suggested Reading," Astrological Texts, p. 203.

Venus/Saturn

Astrologically Venus is ruler of Libra, the sign of balance, harmony, and partnership.[4] Venus represents the energy principle of attraction, love, beauty, and artistry. Saturn is ruler of Capricorn, the sign of ambition, prudence, and government. Saturn represents the energy principle of concentration and inhibition, and is associated with form, structure, hard materials, coldness, and dryness. Personified, Saturn is the enforcer of strict laws and organization.

The effect of their combined influence is observed in the beauty of a crystal where Venus enhances the strictly structured form. Venus confers physical beauty. Saturn gives form, structure and the disciplined arrangement of atoms in space.[5] Venus and Saturn exist together in a snowflake (ice crystal). Saturn cools and restricts moisture. The weather is cold and dry. Snowflakes are restricted, or diminished in size by the contracting, drying principle of Saturn—the cooler and drier the weather, the finer the snow. In wintertime, when the influence of Saturn is modified by Venus, the day is filled with beauty—the snow sparkles in the sunshine and glitters like diamonds. The weather changes dramatically when the influence of Jupiter is introduced. Personified as the rain god, Jupiter represents the energy principles of expansion, abundance, and excess. The effect increases moisture and expands the influence of Venus and Saturn. Huge snowflakes begin to fall which increase in size and number and fill the sky with enormous beauty. It snows all day! The combined influence is often wet and heavy snow before the snowflakes turn into rain and Saturn's influence, the crystalline form, is gone.[6]

---

4. Ruler of Libra is now in question. See "Suggested Reading," on page 203: *Persephone is Transpluto*.

5. Gemologists, jewelers, people interested in jewelry often have Venus/Saturn links in their natal pattern.

6. Personal Observation: Winter in Whistler, British Columbia, 1990-1991. See February 6th and following days. In terms of cosmic energy and the weather, the influence of the sun in winter is the least (Northern Hemisphere) so that the effect of Venus and Saturn is in combination with reduced solar energy. Sun/Saturn limited energy; cold weather. Sun/Venus and Saturn, beauty in cold weather. Venus/Saturn in summer; a cooling trend. Venus/Jupiter in summer, warm rain. In the hierarchical order Venus/Jupiter/Saturn, Venus and Jupiter take precedence and dominate. Saturn's influence is diminished. See drawing page 67.

Venus/Neptune

When Venus is linked with Neptune, the effect is quite different.

Neptune is ruler of Pisces, the sign of compassion, sensitivity, and imagination. Representing the energy principle of reactivity, impressions, and images, Neptune is associated with uncertainty, the unknown, and impossible extremes, like the ideal that is never attained. In negative expression, Neptune's influence is responsible for deception, confusion, and concealment. Neptune's influence spoils things.

Venus and Neptune combine in a beautiful illusion: ideal love; artistic perfection. Venus makes Neptune beautiful. Neptune extends beauty beyond perfect extremes, or spoils it (marred beauty). The effect of their combined influence is observed in a colorful bacterial colony which fascinates, and is quite beautiful in itself, yet hides a harmful toxin and spoils human food.

Response

The effect of cosmic energy is caused by the response of natal patterns to forces created by cosmic bodies in motion. Thus, cosmic energy exerts its influence and has its effect through changing energy focus points.

Everything which occurs on Earth is a response to cosmic energy and, therefore, a record of a cosmic configuration in a particular moment. Beginning with the cosmic arrangement which determines the natal pattern, a cosmic configuration is the precursor of everything which happens: volcanic eruptions, earthquakes, scientific discoveries.

In every single moment of every single night and day, the prevailing cosmic configuration brings energy principles together which influence everything on Earth. As different arrangements occur in the cosmos, the energy influences change. The effect is directly linked with natal pattern responses. These responses determine what happens in the moment. The effect is specific because each natal pattern is unique.

For all things on Earth, one particular cosmic configuration creates its essential pattern.

Lunar Influence

Lunar energy is always exerting its influence—in principle, in transit through alignment, and in configuration. In principle, the moon is about feelings. The moon recommends the attitudes we may not have, but ought to adopt for the best use of the moment.

The energy which emanates continually from cosmic bodies is sometimes described as background energy. The moon collects this background energy and focuses it back to Earth, causing an energy influence to build. The influence builds to full potential at the degree of perfect alignment, and is then released. In this way the moon intensifies, or augments, the energy effect. Since the moon itself has an influence, the lunar principle is always involved in the total cosmic energy expression. Due to the relatively fast movement of the moon through its cycle, a lunar rhythm becomes very well established within all things on Earth.

The moon is always bringing different energy principles into focus at alignment. During the lunar cycle as the moon forms a different angular relationship to each cosmic body, alignments bring prevailing cosmic influences to full potential. This background energy influences all things on Earth. The effect is global.

When the moon is in transit to natal positions (sensitive points in natal patterns) the effect is specific to the pattern. Since the moon is a relatively fast-moving body, it makes connections frequently and is, therefore, constantly activating all natal patterns. The moon triggers everything into motion. Simply stated, a sensitive point in a natal pattern is influenced by the energy principle which occupied that position at birth. When the moon transits a natal position, it causes individual expression according to the moon and the natal principle involved. For example, the transit of the moon (feelings) to natal Saturn (restriction) reflects the principle of self-control (a restriction of feelings). It is a temporary influence because the moon will quickly move out of alignment to this sensitive point. In contrast, Saturn's cycle is slow. The transit of Saturn to the natal moon lasts much longer and has a more profound effect. In reality, transits to natal positions affect the whole pattern and are therefore, more complex.

Thus it is the lunar influence which activates the daily energy, favorably or otherwise, and brings into alignment the multitude of natal patterns for energy expression. The path of the moon is, therefore, very significant.

Lunar Influence

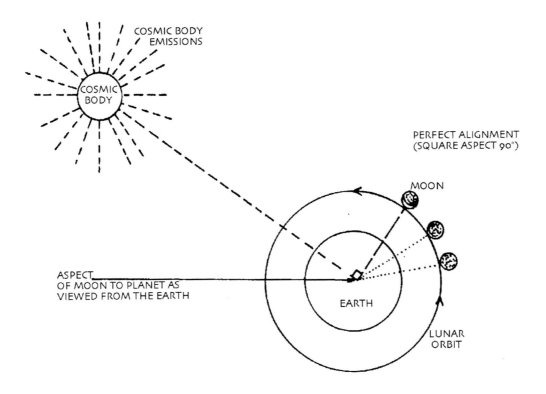

COSMIC BODY
EMISSIONS

COSMIC
BODY

PERFECT ALIGNMENT
(SQUARE ASPECT 90°)

MOON

ASPECT
OF MOON TO PLANET AS
VIEWED FROM THE EARTH

EARTH

LUNAR
ORBIT

The Moon is a Primary Focus

This symbolic illustration shows the path of the moon. Gradually the moon moves into perfect alignment, bringing particular cosmic energy principles into focus. The specific degree at which perfect alignment occurs affects all natal patterns with a sensitive point at that degree. For example, 22° Capricorn or 292° in the zodiac. For other natal patterns, the aspect is a background influence or mood.

Solar/Lunar Exchange

Of particular importance is the relationship between the sun and the moon; the two are inseparable. This causes a quantitative solar-lunar effect. The sun, representing the male principle, and the moon, representing the female principle, combine in a rhythm of solar-lunar exchanges. As the moon reflects solar energy towards the Earth, different phases of the moon intensify the effect. It is through important sun/moon connections that our relationships function. Compatible solar-lunar energy is essential for harmony because it balances the male/female polarities.[1] Within the interplay of this polarity, the drama of life unfolds.

---

1. See "Polarity" on page 156.

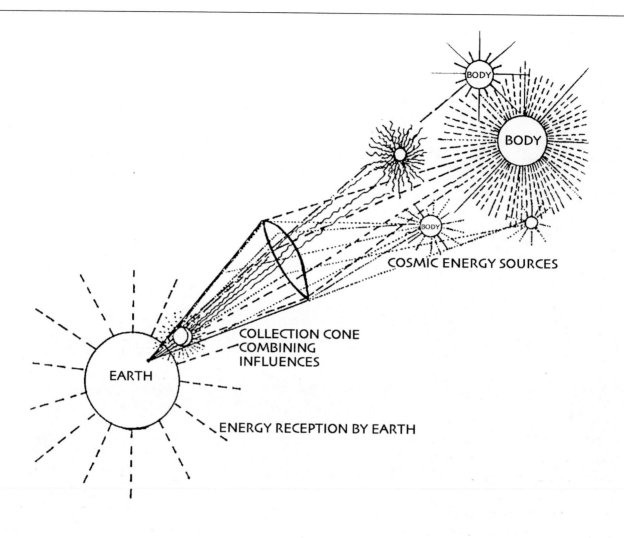

COSMIC ENERGY SOURCES

COLLECTION CONE
COMBINING
INFLUENCES

EARTH

ENERGY RECEPTION BY EARTH

Focus Through the Moon

The illustration shows Earth and the mechanism of energy focus through the moon. Cosmic body sources exert forces which are sensed according to individual natal patterns. The moon acts as an augmentation device which creates sufficient focus to trigger events on Earth. Energy builds, or increases, to the point of alignment and is then released. Thus, the effect of cosmic energy is felt prior to alignment like an incoming wave before it crashes on the beach.

Cycle Frequency

When a planet moves very slowly around the sun, it remains in an orb of influence to a position on the Earth for some time. The slower the cycle, the more prolonged the influence. For this reason, slowly moving bodies such as Neptune have long term influences. Rapidly moving bodies such as Mercury, which skips around quickly, have a fleeting effect.

Clarification

There is a difference between an aspect and a transit. An aspect within a natal pattern affects the individual. It is permanent or lifelong. An aspect in the cosmos affects everyone and everything. The effect is global, although individual response varies.

A transit to a natal position affects the individual. Transits are passing influences and, therefore, temporary. Whenever any cosmic body transits a sensitive point in a natal pattern, an energy influence is brought into play causing a specific cosmic/natal interaction. Two planets in particular angular relationship in the cosmos without another influence, express energy according to the two principles involved. When the combined cosmic influence aligns with a sensitive point, natal principles are included. The lunar influence adds a fourth principle and brings everything to full potential during alignment.

Interpretation: Moon/Venus/Saturn

The effect of cosmic bodies involves position.

When Venus in transit[7] arrives at the sensitive point occupied by natal Saturn, the energy effect is a combination of both principles—Venus is tempered by Saturn. When the moon also aspects that point, it is not only a moon/Saturn principle in effect, but temporarily a moon, Venus, Saturn influence and, thus, involves the mesh of all three principles. As Venus moves away or separates, natal Saturn is once again the only influence in that position and exerts its effect according to the natal pattern. The orb of influence is considered to be five degrees prior to perfect alignment. Depending on the nature of the energy involved, very little effect is felt following separation.[8]

It should be noted that not all sensitive points exert a single or simple effect. Strong aspects from other natal positions have an effect at all times, so that for most patterns certain energy influences always work together.

7. Transit. See Glossary, page 212.
8. See "Suggested Reading," page 203: Astrological Texts.

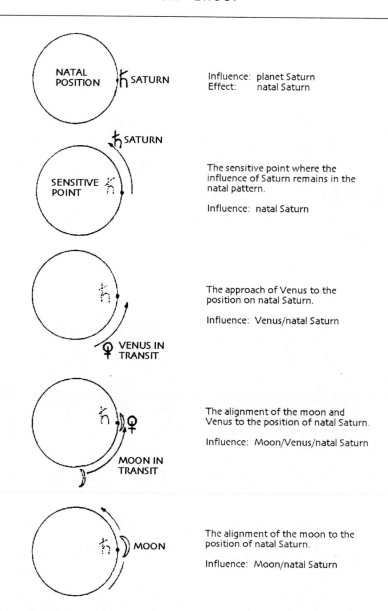

NATAL POSITION ♄ SATURN	Influence: planet Saturn Effect: natal Saturn
♄ SATURN SENSITIVE POINT	The sensitive point where the influence of Saturn remains in the natal pattern. Influence: natal Saturn
VENUS IN TRANSIT	The approach of Venus to the position on natal Saturn. Influence: Venus/natal Saturn
MOON IN TRANSIT	The alignment of the moon and Venus to the position of natal Saturn. Influence: Moon/Venus/natal Saturn
MOON	The alignment of the moon to the position of natal Saturn. Influence: Moon/natal Saturn

The natal position of a cosmic body is very important because it determines the overall influence of that body in the natal pattern. The influence at a sensitive point is always included in the response to the cosmos. It determines the manner of pattern connection and is included in the total energy effect. This diagram shows a few of the subtle changes in influence at a particular position. The example shown is natal Saturn.

) ♀ ♄ Astrological symbols for Moon, Venus, Saturn.

Portrait of Saturn

Saturn is a controlling influence in the cosmos.

The effect of Saturn on Earth is observed in different ways: through limitation, restriction, separation, denial, responsibility, delay, and endurance. Humans experience insufficient funds; limited facilities; confinement due to poor health, or feebleness in old age; imprisonment; absence of people, which denies opportunity through lack of contact; isolation causing loneliness; heavy responsibilities which delay personal progress; long, hard struggles for success.

Cosmic energy is unlimited and ubiquitous. Limits are caused by restrictive patterns. Saturn in a pattern is a limiting influence which delays and can prevent connection. In cosmic terms, energy is restricted which affects the moment in various ways: prolonged or slow expression of energy; delayed interaction; limited connection and, therefore, expression. The influence of Saturn in a moment is how the cosmos controls natal patterns for the purpose of destiny and karma.[9]

Form and structure are associated with Saturn.

Hydrogen oxide in its solid state (ice) cannot pass through a tiny aperture. In its liquid state, water easily passes through. Ice is restricted by its structural form. The influence of Saturn controls the shape of ice by limiting energy, which prevents the change of state to water.

Saturn is a separating influence.

Saturn controls connection through the principles of delay and separation. If patterns are not brought together, interaction does not occur. By causing delay and, thereby, preventing connection until a particular alignment has passed, Saturn separates through timing.[10] For this reason, Saturn is often considered to be the timer within the solar system. Saturn's cycle is, therefore, very important. The influence of Saturn is observed in everyday life: when a person misses the last bus and is forced to walk home; in having to work late at the office and forego a dinner party; in being separated from others due to responsibility. One feels restricted, limited, controlled by something.

Saturn delays.

Saturn is a delaying influence, an effect experienced as a time factor. In human terms, it means waiting. The feeling that nothing is happening is really being in a limited energy expression—a moment dominated by Saturn. Time seems to drag. The individual experiences waiting. No one who has not experienced a Saturn transit really comprehends the meaning of slow—it seems to take forever! On a cosmic time scale, human delay is but a fleeting moment. To the individual it may seem like eternity itself. When delay occurs so that natal patterns connect in a particular way, Saturn is controlling destiny through synchronicity which involves karma itself.[11]

---

9. See "Lifepath" on page 184; and "Perspective" on page 188.
10. See "Twelve• Synchronicity" on page 154.

Saturn causes denial.

The inability to enjoy particular moments through Saturn's influence causes the individual to experience denial. This is not self-denial, but cosmic denial.

Saturn creates the feeling of loneliness.

Without ever having been alone is not to have experienced separation and isolation. To be alone but not lonely, describes solitude, and is a function of being apart from others. To be lonely is to feel cut off from others, or separated from where one might prefer to be. One may feel lonely in a crowd, which is beyond the physical experience; it has to do with emotion. One also may feel intellectually lonely, isolated from mental rapport. Whenever loneliness comes, the influence of Saturn is involved. Personified, Saturn is often depicted as Old Man Winter: grey-bearded, wrinkled and thin, a bag of bones, tired, lonely and impoverished. He is the old man who shuffles slowly before us to the ticket booth, preventing our getting past him and forcing us to wait in turn.

Saturn forces natal patterns to learn.

In everyday life the figure of Saturn is also the disciplinarian, the one who causes us to learn. For most of us, that person is the school teacher who makes us study; the doctor who makes us exercise when we feel lazy or forces us to rest when we wish to be active; the parent who tells us to tidy a room. None of this is bad, but at the time we often feel restricted by discipline. Under the influence of Saturn, cosmic energy is usually forced to express in a particular way as a result of limitation. In this context the effect is control. Thus, the cosmos is an invisible teacher. Through the energy principles of Saturn, each natal pattern learns, teaches, and is taught. A lifetime is the space in which we are shown.

---

11. See "Karmic Recoding" on page 190.

Portrait of Uranus

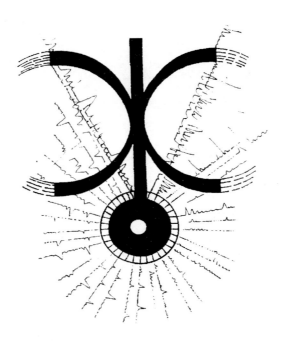

Uranus is the Harbinger of Change.

Cosmic energy expressed through Uranian influence is always associated with change: the unexpected, the unusual, and, most frequently, suddenness. All of a sudden, as if from nowhere, things change, yet the agent of change is gone, has moved on, leaving behind a fresh set of circumstances as energy rearranges itself. In this way Uranus is a neutral principle, like a catalyst which sets everything into motion without itself becoming involved.

Uranus turns things around.

Neutral in its expression, Uranus is the principle of reversal. This effect is observed in a traffic incident in which a vehicle suddenly spins around on the road. Not infrequently the driver and the vehicle are unharmed. Most often, such an incident is a catalyst which causes other vehicles to swerve creating chaos: death, injury, wreckage. It illustrates the element of neutrality where Uranus causes sudden reversal. The effect is an upset in smoothly flowing, daily events. Although what happens when Uranus turns everything around and upside-down in sudden, unexpected ways may be observed as a delightful surprise, it is mostly witnessed as an upsetting event. In cosmic terms, it is part of the larger order of things. In everyday existence, it is the prelude to change. What is vertical may become horizontal. A bridge collapses into the water and cannot be repaired; a new bridge must be built. In one moment some people are riding in a car, in the next they are dead. What is active and vital is altered forever. At once everything is changed for the next of kin; life for them seems ruined.

Change due to Uranus is irreversible, which creates the opportunity for a new direction.

Uranus forces energy patterns to evolve.

Uranus is responsible for mutation which is the pre-requisite for evolution. Without Uranian energy, evolution cannot take place. Patterns which allow new thinking and new ways direct the choices we make. Successful patterns direct cosmic energy. Gradually evolution occurs as these patterns come into being. The effect may be considered in terms of discoveries and inventions: the wheel; the internal combustion engine; the computer. In this way Uranus is the planet of invention, bringing new things into existence. Personified, Uranus is the awakener, the person who enters one's life and influences it as never before, and in whatever way is necessary for individual development in the fulfillment of destiny. For most individuals, that person is often a mentor.

Uranus is instantaneous.

Uranus represents the circuitry within a pattern and, like electrical wiring, allows instant connection. When Uranian transits occur, a cosmic energy influence suddenly comes into play which is both unexpected and immediate, like the ring of a telephone, a sudden explosion, an earthquake.

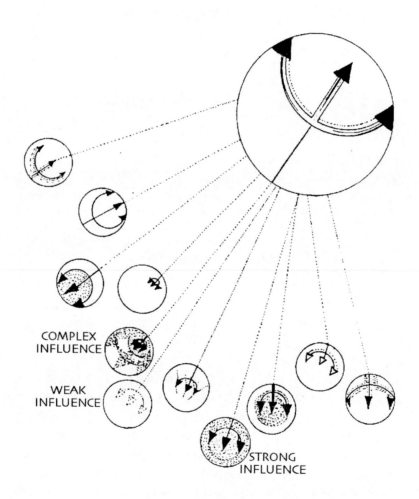

Each cosmic body is represented in every natal pattern because each body is part of every cosmic configuration. Neptune has been selected to illustrate this concept.

In this illustration the artist depicts planet Neptune linked to each natal pattern where the astrological symbol of Neptune is drawn differently in each circle to portray natal pattern differences. The arrangement of energy alignments between the position of Neptune and other cosmic bodies determines the global effect of Neptune's influence in each cosmic configuration. In the same way internal energy links between the position of natal Neptune and other natal positions determine how Neptune influences each pattern. For this reason some patterns are more responsive to emissions from Neptune than others.

Portrait of Neptune

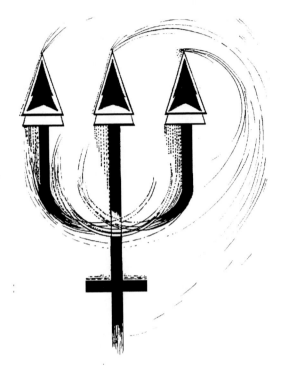

Neptune likes to conceal.
Neptune represents the hidden—secrets, private places.

Neptune gradually moves around the sun. Its cycle is slow; its influence long lasting and far reaching. The effect is like a mist which hangs around keeping things secret. Neptune's influence is observed in the summer mist on the ocean—the barely visible vapor distorting distance, enhancing beauty, and the dense impenetrable fog, denying direction, concealing entirely. Between these two extremes lies the energy realm of Neptune, the influence which conceals and only reveals in part. Something always remains unknown. Other cosmic body influences often cause a more obvious effect so that the presence of Neptune goes unnoticed. Neptune, nevertheless, contributes in the subtle way that conceals, clouds, distorts, exaggerates, and extends. Neptune is always in the background and is to be acknowledged.

Neptune lingers.

Waiting, yet not appearing to do so, is an energy effect of Neptune. It is like the spider waiting in its web; like the pregnant woman waiting for the child to be born; like the ovum waiting to be fertilized. This facet of Neptune is personified in the oaf who loiters; the prostitute who lingers in the streets; the drunkard who hangs around the pub. Waiting due to Neptune is different from Saturn's influence, which causes waiting through *delay.*

Neptune is a nuisance.

Neptune's influence is felt as a nuisance. It is the irritating sound that punctuates the silence: the dripping tap, the wasp trapped by the window pane, the dog which whines. Humans experience a blister on a heel, an ill-fitting shoe, a sliver in a finger which causes pain. Personified, the effect of irritation is observed in the nagging spouse.

Neptune pollutes.

Associated with chemicals, oils, and gases, the effect of Neptune includes obscurity and disappearance. Things tend to be uncertain, smudged as in a smoke screen. It is observed in the candle that disappears as the wick burns, the burning fuel in automobile engines that seems to disappear in exhaust fumes.

Pollution is a negative expression of Neptune's influence: waste materials, refuse, rubbish, invisible vehicle exhausts, unwanted industrial emissions, the dirty environment. Smog—at one time the word did not exist. Now, barely discernible beneath the smog, cities are ghosts in the daylight.

Astrology Shows that Cosmic Energy Principles Influence the Weather

The heat of the sun is diminished under the influence of Saturn, which exerts a cooling effect by restricting solar power. The heat of the sun is augmented by the influence of Mars and Jupiter. The energy of Mars is increased by Jupiter so that the influence of the sun is increased in heat, light, and intensity. There is excess solar energy. The effect on Earth is a scorching sun. The light of the sun is obscured by Neptune which conceals. The sun is hazy, the horizon distorted, definition disappears[12]

Neptune's Revenge

> *Therefore, the winds, piping to us in vain,*
> *As in revenge, have sucked up from the sea*
> *Contagious fogs; which falling in the land,*
> *Having every pelting river made so proud,*
> *That they have overborne their continents.*
>
> William Shakespeare
> *A Midsummer Night's Dream*

---

12. Personal Observations: Although not researched in detail the author in her many years as a landscape designer observed these astrological links with the weather. See page 54: Venus, Saturn.

Literature, poetry, and, more recently, scientific records describe adverse weather phenomena, which in the past were not infrequently attributed to angry gods. In Greek mythology, Zeus (Jupiter) the rain god and Poseidon (Neptune) god of the oceans, personified two of these forces.

In terms of mythological whimsy, Jupiter is being confronted by Neptune.[13] It is not a favorable exchange. Neptune is claiming dues. Water is leaving the land; less rain falls at the expected time, too much falls when it is not needed, or wanted and runs away. All over the world there is less water in the land. Rivers are less full; lakes are lower; reservoirs are shrinking; creek beds dry out for longer periods; high altitudes retain less snow; ice is disappearing; mountain peaks are bare for longer; wells run dry. Everywhere water is returning to the sea. It is the time of Neptune's revenge.

Revenge includes all things Neptunian: oil, drugs, bacteria, pesticides, chemicals. The oceans have been treated as the waste baskets of the world. What humans no longer want is dumped into the ocean, or finds its way there through polluted rivers and water systems. Dumping refuse into the Earth's water systems is an insult to Neptune, who is beginning to retaliate. Insidiously these unwanted wastes are being returned to the human species, as films of oil on sea water that slowly creep ashore to coat the rocks and clog the feathers of seabirds; in toxic fish; in smog enshrouded cities; pesticide residues in vegetables; contaminated drinking water; drugs and diseases in human bloodstreams. Pollution is everywhere. It has crept into everything through insidious infiltration and seepage.

In selfish, thoughtless, careless greed, humans have exploited and abused the hidden, the private places belonging to Neptune: ore bodies, fossil fuel reserves.

Neptune whispers to the human race:

> *For too long you have abused my realms…*
> *I am private. You have lost respect for privacy.*
> *I shall invade your most private places…*
> *I shall spoil things. I shall return the pollutants…*
> *To your drinking water, to the air you breathe.*
> *I shall fill your cities with drugs and your people with disease.*
> *I shall contaminate your blood….*

In cosmic terms, universal law demands energy balance—debts must be repaid. The effect is observed in restoring equilibrium. The world has wasted water. Now water is laying waste the land as Neptune reflects Jupiter's greed.

---

13. At the time of writing. Reference: Mississippi Floods of 1993.

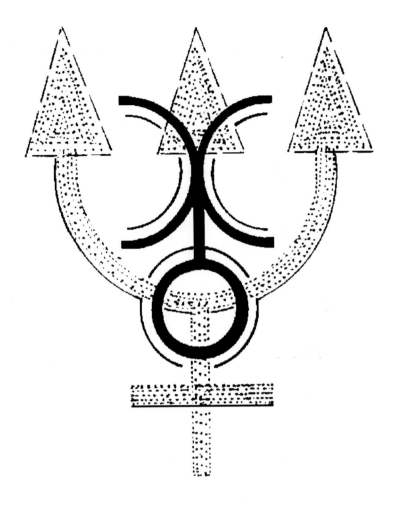

Uranus/Neptune Conjunction: 171-Year Cycle

PRINCIPLE   Freedom From Illusion, Knowing

                     Changing the Visual Image: A Sudden Clarity Of Vision

                     Breaking Familiar Ideals: An Awakening To Reality

                     A Change From Illusion, Non-reality

EFFECT   The Broken Illusion

                     The Shattered Image

When energy is focused towards a particular degree for a long time, the alignment is an energy shaft that behaves like an axis about which other cosmic energy revolves.[14]

---

14. See "Cosmic Energy Axis" on page 5.

Three times in 1993, Uranus and Neptune were in conjunction aspect in Capricorn. The orb of their combined influence was between 18° and 22°. One of the energy principles of this combination is knowing, or cognition—literally, a freedom from illusion. The effect of Neptune is to muddy, distort, and conceal not only the things we want to see and know, but those that we prefer remain hidden, including the things we hide even from ourselves. In conjunction with Uranus, Neptune was forced to purify, clarify, and reveal. In 1993 unpredictable Uranian energy upset and exposed Neptune's influence, which tends to hide the evidence and to cover up through veils of secrecy. In cosmic dialogue:

Neptune	"I like to keep things hidden."
Uranus	"I want to be free. When I am tangled with you I am not free. I shall upset everything until my involvement with you is released."
Neptune	"I will hide your unruly behavior."
Uranus	"I don't care. I shall expose your secrets so that you dare not show your face."
Neptune	"I will confuse you in mist, and flood water over your traces."

Neptune always has the last word.

Throughout 1993, Uranus and Neptune approached, aligned, and receded from each other, like a swivel. Because these two planets move so slowly and were very closely aligned, the subtle difference in effect caused by the changes in their positions might not have been noticed. The influence was felt and observed in many ways.

As Uranus approached Neptune, the global effect was observed as a sudden, unexpected event involving water, gas, or chemicals. Underground pipelines suddenly ruptured releasing gas. Unexpected flooding undermined houses. A sudden mine explosion trapped miners underground (hidden by Neptune).[15] A train suddenly went off the tracks, spilling toxic chemicals, causing evacuation of a town.

After alignment there was a subtle energy change because their respective positions reversed. As Uranus receded from Neptune, the effect was a freedom from illusion, a sudden perception. A misled public was suddenly made aware so that a way of thinking (belief system) changed. Private lives were suddenly exposed. For some it meant that an individual wish, secret hope, or dream was suddenly shattered, a promise broken. This was mainly experienced as a sudden jolt, like an electric shock, followed by a changed awareness of reality. It is best described as a broken image or shattered illusion.

In summary, all over the Earth many things were not as they appeared to be. This energy influence merely brought them into the moment and broke the illusion. All events were associated with a neutral factor and a subtle, hidden element resulting in sudden change which, for many, was very disruptive. The effect of the conjunction was in existence for over two years.

For too long the world has been under an illusion.
Uranus, the awakener, has given us the freedom to know through enlightenment—we are controlled
by cosmic energy through our natal pattern.
Whatever we may think, or believe, choices exist only at certain times.
Destiny is all patterned out.

---

15. See Westray Mine Disaster (Canada) in Appendix, "Uranus/Neptune Conjunction 1993: Interpretation" on page 205.

What is seen is the effect of cosmic energy.
What is not seen are the forces which cause things to happen.

The MV BRAER

In January 1993, the oil tanker MV BRAER went aground in Sumburgh, Scotland. Television pictures showed a huge vessel fast on the rocks, jammed between land and sea, in the worst place for any ship—a rocky shore in a storm. Pounded by relentless waves and lashing winds, the abandoned ship MV BRAER was paralyzed in the grip of death. Oil escaped into the water as the hull began to leak. Another oil disaster occurred when the storm turned into a gale and the ship broke apart.

In cosmic terms, Sumburgh is the death position for MV BRAER, the energy focus point on Earth where cosmic interaction with the ship's natal pattern caused a tragedy for the world, and Sumburgh, in particular. At that time, incoming energy emissions from the Uranus/Neptune conjunction caused a sudden change in energy that disrupted the influence of several other cosmic bodies. The influence of the prevailing cosmic configuration was strengthened during the full moon, causing the powerful energy directions which prevented MV BRAER from continuing its voyage and sustaining its shape.[16]

The event was sudden, unexpected, and upsetting (Uranus) involving oil and the sea (Neptune). Typical of Neptune's influence, the effect lingered after the event. The oil spread a film over the sea and shoreline, destroying a wildlife habitat. Infiltrating fumes crept insidiously over the land so that the island inhabitants felt ill. A world watched in tragic dismay.

Watching television is like watching a replay of cosmic energy in action.[17]

For millions, watching the disaster through television was like a hidden,
individual involvement made possible by a neutral element, television (Uranus), and illustrates
Neptune's far-reaching influence.[18]

The Daily Influence

The next time you go for a walk, ask yourself if you really made the decision, or was another force causing you to move? The next time you drink some wine or wash your hands, perhaps the moon is linking with Neptune, or natal Neptune in your pattern. The next time you see an old person, or the doctor, or someone alone, perhaps Saturn's influence is in the background. The next time your telephone rings, remember Uranus.

---

16. See Appendix, page 206, Table 1.
17. See "The Second Dimension" on page 132.
18. See "Portrait of Neptune" on page 65.

Seven • Movement

FLUX

Nothing stays the same...change is inevitable.

Cosmic energy is in a perpetual state of flux.

Within this flux, all things exist;
all things have their moment;
all things happen...and pass.

Perpetual movement, the state of flux, is the very feature of cosmic energy which underlies change and impermanence. At the same time this energy process of connection, disconnection and reconnection allows an infinite potential for the evolution of energy patterns.

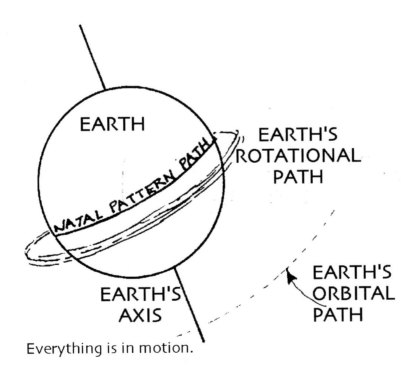

Everything is in motion.

Earth's Rhythm

Cosmic energy is the vital force in the cosmos.

People are part of the Earth. As the Earth moves, people move, even when they are standing still. Every twenty-four hours, as the Earth spins on its axis, all things on Earth turn once in the daily cycle. Every year, as the Earth orbits the sun, all things on Earth revolve once in the yearly cycle. Since the Earth is in constant motion, each position on Earth is also continually moving. This motion is the Earth's rhythm; it is the rotating environment in which all things exist. It causes everything to experience a different position relative to everything else. This movement is the pre-requisite which allows cosmic energy interactions among patterns in the continuum of energy cycles. In this way cosmic energy passes through the days and years for all of us. Like a wind in the trees, it passes through and affects us all.

BACKGROUND ENERGY EMITTED FROM ALL COSMIC BODIES

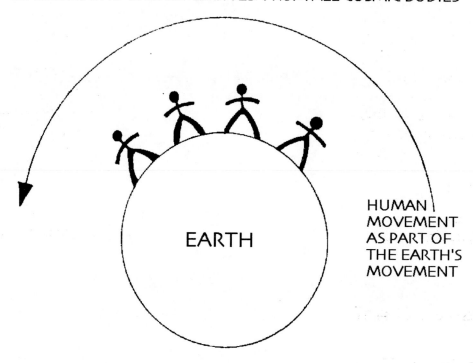

EARTH

HUMAN
MOVEMENT
AS PART OF
THE EARTH'S
MOVEMENT

Human Movement as Part of the Earth's Movement

This illustration shows a person (pin figure) moving with the Earth. Individual movement such as walking, swimming, or dancing is due to different responses to cosmic energy by each natal pattern.

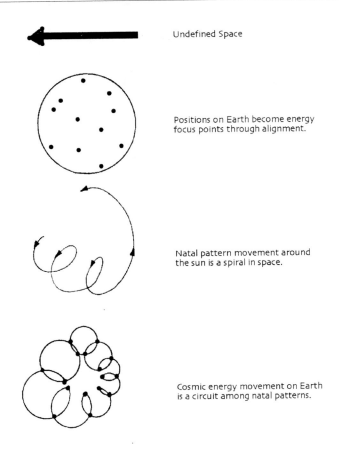

Undefined Space

Positions on Earth become energy focus points through alignment.

Natal pattern movement around the sun is a spiral in space.

Cosmic energy movement on Earth is a circuit among natal patterns.

Cosmic Rhythm

Cosmic energy movement is a cyclical rhythm.

Cosmic rhythm is the background rhythm for everything. In order to fully understand this rhythm and cosmic energy in particular, it is necessary to break the habit of lineal perception. Not only has the huge emphasis on reading and writing from a very early age conditioned the human brain to lineal movement, but also most humans consider the passage of time as a lineal concept, in which time is thought to pass and, once passed, never returns. In fact, time does not pass. Energy moves into space.[1] Furthermore, the movement is cyclical, not lineal.

Cosmic energy arrangement is determined by cosmic body cycles. The energy patterns which form in the process are, therefore, connected to these cycles. Cosmic body cycles bring energy patterns into existence, synchronize their connection, and cause their disintegration. In this way, cycles control cosmic energy as the energy sources move from one position to another.

The cyclical nature of cosmic bodies allows energy to return and pass through the same dimensions (energy-sensitive shapes) many times.[2] The process permits multidimensional

1. See "Energy Moves into Space" on page 107.

energy connections and interaction. As cosmic comprehension forces a new way of thinking, new concepts will allow humans to direct their own evolution.

Cyclical Interval

Cosmic energy cycles are based on the orbits of cosmic bodies. Each cosmic body cycles at a particular frequency and exerts a specific influence. In this way the cycles may be likened to spinning cog wheels which turn at different rates; all interlock, but some rotate so slowly that particular interconnection is very infrequent.

Cosmic energy cycles are pulses, the frequency of which depends on the cyclical interval. Cycles of long duration, like Neptune, are slow pulses, like very slow heartbeats. Cycles of short duration, like the moon, are rapid, or frequent pulses.

A simple cycle is the duration of one complete orbit of a body around another, for example, the lunar cycle which lasts for about a month. A complex cycle involves two, or more, cosmic bodies which share a relationship at particular intervals. Complexity depends on the number of bodies and includes cycles of relationship and cycles of position.[3] The effect is due to their combined influence. Both simple and complex cycles are single pulses. Cyclical complexity is observed in cycles within cycles, such as the female menstrual cycle in a woman's lifetime. Everything on Earth is affected by cycles and portrays the typical cyclical phenomenon: culmination and decline. It is a rhythm which is observed in many familiar ways: in tides which ebb and flow; in lungs which inhale and exhale; in civilizations which rise and fall.

2. See "Crystalline Corridor" on page 136; and drawings pgs. 142-146.
3. See "Suggested Reading" on page 203: *Astrological Timing*.

Cyclical Phenomena

A cycle is a unit of energy influence.

A cosmic energy cycle is a unit of universal time, a measure of arc-time, the time for completion of orbits specific to the energy principles involved.[4] It is a period, like a time frame, within which particular energy influences manifest. The cycle of the Earth is the most familiar:

Falling leaves in autumn:

> fog~short days~cooling temperatures
> snow~cold winter~hibernation~thaw
> spring~flowers~new leaves~freshness
> sunshine~summer warmth~long days
> heat~lush growth~ripeness~harvest
> darker evenings~magnificent hues~falling leaves in autumn

Cosmic energy influence is observed in other cycles: illness cycles, criminal cycles, learning cycles. The phrase, "It has run its course," is often used in connection with illness, like measles, which goes through an incubation period, manifests, peaks, and declines. The phrase really means the cycle is complete.

Merge Point

Completion is in an energy focus point.

The completion of a cycle is both an ending and a beginning—a merge point, a focus point in space.[5] Like a spinning wheel, another cycle will continue. Nothing actually "begins" or "ends," for all things depend on what preceded them and influence what follows. Merge points are perhaps best described as significant moments. The phrase, when one door closes another opens, expresses this concept in idiomatic terms. Slowly moving cosmic bodies allow merge points to stretch or extend into an arc of parallel movement (parallel timing) so that synchronized timing during slow alignment manifests in a phase of influence. The human experience is a way of life for a period. The arc of the Uranus/Neptune conjunctions in 1993 was a global influence, in which the effect was intensified for particular individuals over a two-year period.

It is within the continuous procession of cycles that humans find their place, their life cycles.

---

4. See Glossary, "Energy Cycle," page 211.
5. See "Merge Point" on page 143.

METAPHYSICAL CONCEPT: Nothing begins; nothing ends.
There is only change in an energy continuum.

Cyclical Links

Planetary cycles interrelate.

Uranus is associated with seven years, the time it takes the planet to pass through one zodiac sign, or an arc of 30°. Although it takes Uranus eighty-four years to complete an orbit around the sun, astrologers usually consider Uranus in seven-year periods. This is partly because Uranus makes a different aspect to its natal position in all natal patterns every seven years. Neptune is associated with fourteen years for similar reasons. Thus, every fourteen years there is an astrological link between Neptune and Uranus. These links involve multiples of seven, where fourteen, twenty-one, twenty-eight, forty-two and fifty-six are very significant ages in human life.

Deciphering cycles is both simple and immediately complex. Uranus and Neptune are partially responsible for cycle obscurity. The Uranian energy principle complicates cycle interpretation because the very nature of Uranian energy turns everything around in unexpected reversal. While Uranus contributes an upsetting element, Neptune conceals by creating uncertainty. In this way the masking nature and slower cycle of Neptune adds complexity to interpretation. In addition, many other cycles are interwoven among these, including much longer cycles that allow repetition of energy patterns that existed in distant antiquity. This may explain why cycle recognition and deciphering has remained elusive for so long.

Uranus/Neptune/Saturn

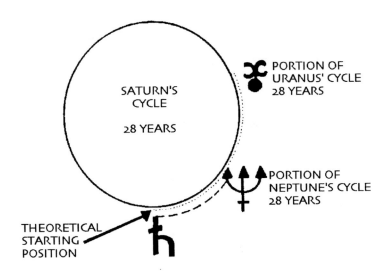

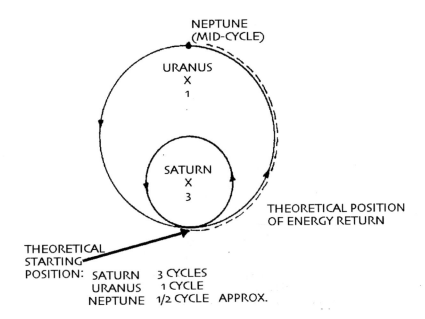

Planetary Cycles Interrelate

This symbolic illustration shows cyclical links among Saturn, Uranus, and Neptune. As Saturn in transit, approaches the natal Saturn position in a birth chart, or natal pattern, the individual is twenty-eight years of age. A full cycle of Saturn for that person is nearing completion. Uranus has moved 120°. Neptune has moved 60°.

Energy Return

Energy cycles allow patterns to reoccur.

The cyclical nature of cosmic energy allows the phenomenon of energy return. It permits a cosmic body to occupy a position in its orbit over and over again, which in turn allows energy principles to recombine and exert an influence. Regardless of the cyclical interval, cyclical movement brings energy principles together again in very similar arrangements. This cosmic energy feature permits energy patterns to reoccur. Similar patterns allow similar energy expression—similar circumstances occur on Earth; similar characters reappear; history repeats itself. The more similar the cosmic arrangement, the more similar the energy expression and, therefore, the greater the similarity of the event on Earth. Similarity is most easily observed when the energy expression leaves an indelible memory imprint. The more unusual, traumatic, or important an event, such as a huge volcanic eruption, a gruesome murder, or a record-setting athletic feat, the less likely the event will be forgotten or go unnoticed the next time around. Such events are very important cycle markers.[6]

Points of cycle completion are known as positions of energy return.

When a cycle brings a cosmic body to its natal position in a pattern, the effect is like a reinforcement of the energy principle. It causes similarity of energy expression as though the natal pattern were restating itself through that principle. In each lifetime each human experiences the phenomenon of energy return. The youthful experience reoccurs in a slightly changed set of circumstances. The cycle markers may be obscure, but will nevertheless be recognizable.

CONCEPT: Similarity occurs at energy return.

---

6. In 1935, Edward VII abdicated from the throne to marry a divorced woman, Wallis Simpson. At the time of writing, Prince Charles may not become king in order to marry Camilla Parker-Bowles. Compare also the striking similarity between Mary, the late Queen Mother, and Diana—both tall, elegant, beautiful, and of similar bearing. (20.01.97)

Similarity

The youthful experience describes similarity at energy return.

Complex cycle interconnection may mask energy return, particularly when long timespans are involved; nevertheless, the cycles and their influences still exist. In general, the less prominent the energy expression, the less recognition it received; events pass unnoticed. The longer the cyclical interval, or time frame, the less obvious the connection, or relationship, of one event to another. The following is a simple example of similarity in which the cyclical interval is almost sixty years.

Moment of energy expression: First Occasion

The grandmother as a young child hiccups while having a piano lesson. The music teacher standing behind the child, slaps the child on the back suddenly. The child cries in fear of reprimand, thinking the piano playing is not good enough. However, the slap is for the hiccups; the tears are unnecessary; the thoughts of the child are private or hidden.

Moment of energy expression: Second Occasion

The young grandchild hiccups repeatedly. The grandmother (who was the child during the first occasion) is reminded of her piano lesson a long time ago and begins to recount her childhood experience. In the same moment the telephone rings. The message is to inform of the death of the piano teacher. Tears ensue again from the grandmother who once again has private thoughts. She inwardly notices a strange coincidence in events.[7]

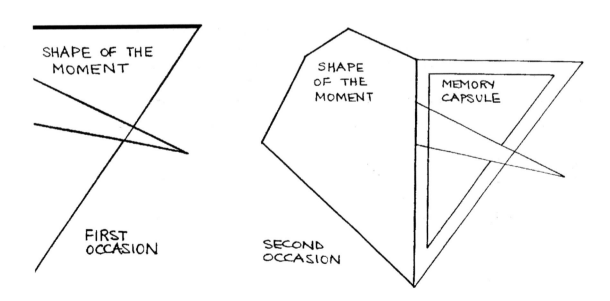

---

7. See: Memory, *Neptune in Focus,* forthcoming.

Cyclical Phenomena: The Youthful Experience

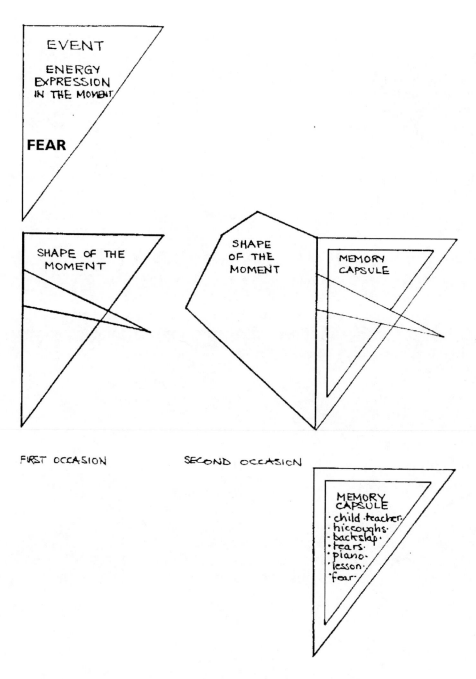

Picture of Energy

The shape for each moment is different because each moment is unique.

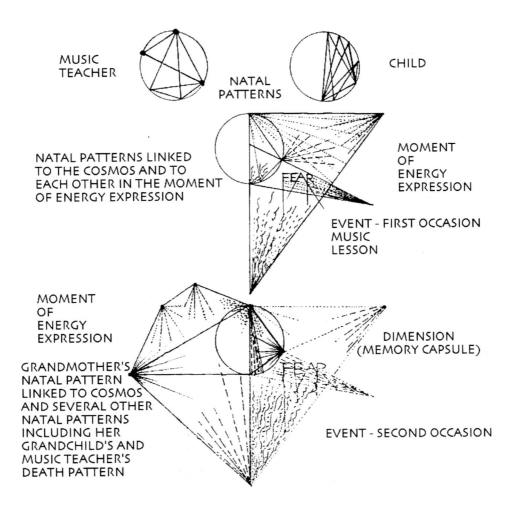

MUSIC
TEACHER

NATAL
PATTERNS

CHILD

NATAL PATTERNS LINKED
TO THE COSMOS AND TO
EACH OTHER IN THE MOMENT
OF ENERGY EXPRESSION

MOMENT
OF
ENERGY
EXPRESSION

FEAR

EVENT - FIRST OCCASION
MUSIC
LESSON

MOMENT
OF
ENERGY
EXPRESSION

GRANDMOTHER'S
NATAL PATTERN
LINKED TO COSMOS
AND SEVERAL OTHER
NATAL PATTERNS
INCLUDING HER
GRANDCHILD'S AND
MUSIC TEACHER'S
DEATH PATTERN

DIMENSION
(MEMORY CAPSULE)

FEAR

EVENT - SECOND OCCASION

The (Grandmother's) Youthful Experience

The hiccups of a grandchild triggers a memory of a childhood music lesson. The diagrams show this as a link with another dimension to be considered as a memory capsule. In the grandmother's experience, the hiccups are a marker on a cycle that links her with the music teacher.

Interpretation

Cycle markers or linking factors:

> the music teacher
> a child and an older person
> neutral objects (piano—telephone)
> a sudden unexpected incident (backslap—telephone call)
> hiccups—tears—private thoughts—suffering
> only the grandmother cried on both occasions.
> no words passed between the music teacher and grandmother on either occasion.

On the first occasion, an unexpected event during a music lesson caused an immediate subconscious fear of reprimand which induced crying through a misunderstanding and a lack of communication. It left an indelible memory.

On the second occasion, the energy cycle which brought hiccups to the grandchild triggered a memory in the grandmother. It coincided with an unexpected telephone call concerning the former music teacher, just as the grandmother is recounting her childhood experience of hiccups and that very person.

Particular principles are linked again. Although cosmic energy is similar, its arrangement is different because most of the cosmic bodies are in different positions so that energy expression on the second occasion results in a different set of circumstances. However, there is sufficient similarity to link the two scenarios together. The main influence is Saturn's return, the alternate Saturn cycle (approximately sixty years). However, Uranian energy, which tends to reverse or turn things the other way around making recognition more difficult, and Neptunian energy, which obscures, are also involved.

All events may be interpreted in this way. The more profound the experience, the more readily and accurate the recall. When cycles are observed, it is easier to recognize similarities. There are many occasions in life when people recount events from the past, unaware that cycles are linking. It is very common among older people who reminisce for younger persons. When memories are shared with others, it is a learning process. Much wisdom is passed from one generation to another in subtle energy cycle links.

CONCEPT: Similarity occurs at energy return.[8]

Patterns are linked to energy cycles.[9]

---

8. If the time frame is measured between particular events in the past and similar more recent events, a period emerges which may be correlated to planetary cycles. In the same way, by using those time frames and projecting them, it is possible to observe what happens in the future. Many things are strikingly similar at cyclical intervals.
9. See: "Suggested Reading," *The Forces of Destiny* by Penny Thornton, on p. 203.

Character Appearance

Past Lives

Character appearance is a cyclical phenomenon.

People on Earth are in their own moment of existence—a dimension which differs from all others. As cosmic energy passes through these individual dimensions, other people appear in one's life.

For each of us the "other" people in our lives, our family, friends, and colleagues, come and go again and again. Their appearance and disappearance is a part of our daily lives that we take for granted. That we meet intermittently may be recognized, but not necessarily correlated, with cosmic body cycles. From time to time, a person appears in our life who is similar to someone whom we have known previously. As we observe the physical likeness, we also notice similarities in associated events in which both timing and details echo the past. As the "expected" characters reappear in one's life, the similarities are strikingly accurate, both in timing and details: the old man with the worn down teeth; the buxom brunette with dark eyes; the girl with a lisp. Animals and inanimate objects such as buildings and clothing also exhibit periodicity and seem to "reappear." The cycle markers are easily recognized in the black and white markings of a cat, the vivid color of a favorite garment, a new white car.[10]

Although recognizable characters corresponding to relatively frequent cycles may be observed in a single lifetime, people representing natal patterns from distant antiquity also return, as and when they should, because infrequent cycles still exist in the background.

The phenomenon of energy return not only allows an individual to examine his life and recall striking similarities at particular times, but also to connect with past lives. At any moment, more than one past life is being linked in the present. Although the current life is predominant in physical reality, nevertheless, an energy connection linking past lives in other dimensions exists and exerts its effect. It is less easily recognized.[11]

10. Personal Observation. This does not refer to the reticular activating system, whereby no sooner than one purchases a car one see those models everywhere.
11. See: "Perspective" on page 124; and "The Ghosts of Destiny" on page 199.

Dissimilarity obscures energy return.

Energy expression is always a combination of influences.[12] In a human lifetime during energy return there is similarity in expression, but it is never quite identical, because other cycles interfere with the pure expression of the energy principle. Usually the bizarre influence of Uranus turns everything around by giving it a twist so that recognition is less obvious. For this reason, energy return may be masked causing difficulty in detection.

Masking is sometimes due to familiarity caused by frequent cycles.[13] As natal patterns rotate with the Earth in the daily cycle, one day is much like another. Most people do not remember daily details which are very similar, but tend to have memories associated with periods, huge numbers of similar moments which merge into a phase of life.

Obscurity is due to dissimilarity. It involves less frequent cycles, such as Saturn, and occurs because cosmic bodies have moved through many more degrees. As a result the prevailing cosmic configuration is significantly different. Usually within a human lifetime, only the returning cosmic body is in its natal position. Lack of recognition is in the human experience and may be attributed to the cyclical interval, Neptune and Uranus. In addition, the alternate cycle involves a considerable number of years which can dim memory recall. Furthermore, Uranus complicates identification through changed expression. Tall and fair may become small and dark; the poor Italian mother may become a wealthy Italian friend.[14]

Overlay or Superimposition

Overlay is a cyclical phenomenon which occurs at energy return. It is the overlay, or superimposition by a moment (energy structure) over the energy sensitive shape of a similar, previous moment in the same position on Earth, and refers to consecutive cyclical events. Overlay is typified in the annual family holiday: a summer vacation at the same time of year with the same people doing the same things in the same place. The holidays are similar enough that they merge in memories: hot, dry weather, and days filled with sunshine, sailing, swimming, walking along the beach. Only particular incidents distinguish them: the time it rained steadily for seven days, the time everyone caught a fish in one afternoon, the time the dinghy capsized. Such events are memory markers, like different dates on similar coins. The concept is presented in terms of stacked coins and is based on the telescope principle.

Frequent superimposition tends to obliterate, as though the energy imprint were smudged which impairs accurate recall.

---

12. See: "The MV BRAER" on page 72.
13. See: "Cycle Overlay: Summer Holidays" on page 88; "Similarity" on page 81; and "Ski-Lift Analogy" on page 108.
14. See: "Energy Reversal" on page 189.

Stacked Coin Analogy

When a number of similar coins are stacked to represent a cylinder, there is one common shape. Each coin, however, is a separate unit of shape. Coin details are not apparent in the stacked position, but are clearly visible when separated. Where a coin cylinder represents a series of summer holidays, each coin may be likened to one holiday. In terms of cosmic energy, each coin is a particular energy expression, a moment which manifests as a summer holiday. At the cyclical interval (one year) another coin is added. Year by year, the number of coins increases. Each coin is superimposed upon all the others. It may be imagined in the form of a stack that collapses into a single coin in which all the energy imprints exist. It is termed energy overlay or superimposition. At the point of cycle overlay, the total energy expression is the sum of the moment and similar dimensions. These merge to give a complex energy imprint to that particular shape in space.[15]

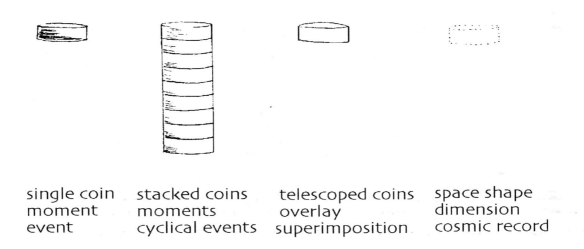

single coin	stacked coins	telescoped coins	space shape
moment	moments	overlay	dimension
event	cyclical events	superimposition	cosmic record

In terms of cosmic energy expression, each moment is different because the positions of cosmic bodies are always changing.

In terms of defined space, there is one extremely similar shape which contains all the moments in the form of dimensions. During overlay, each moment is so similar that only details are slightly different. Only each dimension is a perfect replica of energy expression and distinguishes one moment from another.[16]

15. See "Psychic Phenomena" on page 147.
16. See: "Ski-Lift Analogy" on page 108, and Diagram on page 109.

Cycle Overlay: Summer Holidays

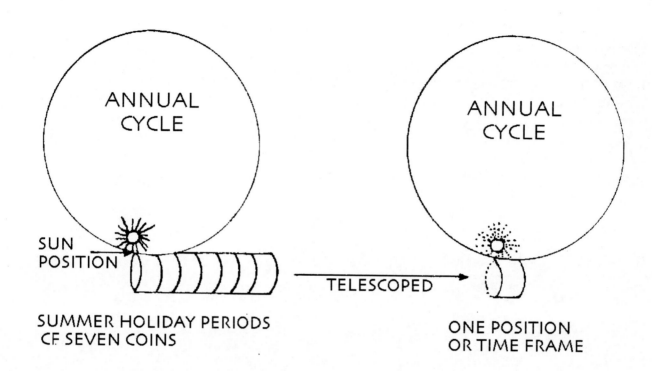

Summer Holidays

This is a symbolic illustration of cycle overlay. Annual summer holidays are cited as an example. Each holiday is a moment—a period of summer fun in the same place with the same people at the same time of year. Each moment occupies the same position in the yearly cycle, and is represented by a shape in space in which cosmic energy is expressed. The moments are illustrated as seven coins. The holidays are, of course, in sequence, like a stack of coins, but in terms of cosmic energy in space, the holidays occupy one position or time frame. It is the energy imprint that is different and distinguishes one holiday from another. Each holiday remains forever in its own dimension, but from a human perspective, events blur after a while. There is a general memory associated with the place, the people, and the time of year. Dimension distinction depends on individual memory ability. [17]

Juxtaposition

Different cycles exhibit different frequencies.

Different cyclical intervals result in juxtaposition which allows historical parallels, but not identical occurrences. Similarity is due to energy return, because similar energy arrangements account for similar energy expression and, therefore, similar events on Earth. Repetition of events on Earth is directly proportional to the similarity of energy arrangement in the cosmos. Variation in what happens on Earth is due to juxtaposition, which refers to the altered arrangement of the cosmos at energy return. Even slightly

---

17. See "Ski-Lift Analogy" on page 108, and "The Sixth Dimension" on page 133.

changed cosmic arrangements create different energy influences so that the energy expression and its effect are also different.

Neptune's energy influence is mostly responsible for masking and obscuring details so that similarity may be observed, but not necessarily linked to any particular past event. Juxtaposition and the Uranian principle, which causes change and reversal, explain why events do not happen in exactly the same way again. Nevertheless, at regular cyclical intervals there is a striking similarity to what happened before. Similar events occur because cosmic energy is arranged once again in a very similar way, allowing particular principles to predominate.

Similar things surround one. Although our residence and living area may have changed, the physical description of the building and our environment are very similar.

Similar characters reappear. Although occupations and mannerisms belonging to friends do not necessarily match in the same way, similar physical types appear in one's life.

A sequence of similar events reoccurs. A new job is once again followed by a change in residence and the purchase of land. The excitement of designing a new house coincides with a successful career.

Character and object appearances represent cycle markers.

Cycle Convergence

Important events and phases in life occur during cycle convergence.

Deciphering cycles is analogous to a jigsaw puzzle—the pieces are all there and only need to be fitted together. Cycles elude easy comprehension only because there are so many to consider. In human experience when cycles converge, it is often observed as an amalgamation: a fusion of several events and characters; a merging into one; a conglomeration; a collage; a collection of many things previously experienced. Recognition of the various cycles in a lifetime serves to illustrate the cyclical nature of cosmic energy. This offers an opportunity to comprehend the deeper meaning of existence, which in itself is also cyclical since it depends on cosmic energy. Physical existence comes and goes, as do the various cosmic configurations because cycles continue to bring cosmic bodies together in particular arrangements. Patterns continue to form; it is a cosmic process in an energy continuum.

Energy Continuum

Cycles determine when things happen.

A circle is the lovely shape of a ring whose simple beauty symbolizes an inner belief in continuity, of continuum. A circle represents strength, for it allows energy to flow evenly around forever by the very nature of its shape. Cosmic cycles are energy inclusive in the same way; they contain energy through the nature of the revolving process. The flow is a continuum of an energy influence over a period. This inclusive process continues until a disruption shatters the strength afforded by the circular, or elliptical, shape. At that time, another influence comes into existence which heralds the dawn of a new era.

CONCEPT: Cosmic energy moves in a cyclical continuum.

Within the cyclical continuum of cosmic body movement,
all things occur;
all things have their moment and pass

Vibration

A cosmic cycle is an energy pulse.

Each cosmic body is associated with a particular cycle frequency. The moon takes a month to orbit the Earth; the Earth takes a year to go round the sun; several planets take many years to complete their orbits. Complex cycles, involving more than one cosmic body, span hundreds of years.[18] Events linked to such cycles belong to eras in human history and may be observed more easily in retrospect. In both simple and complex cycles, the energy principle remains intact so that each energy cycle has a particular influence on Earth.

A cycle of long duration is like a very slow heartbeat or a very slow pulse—an infrequent vibration that exists in the background. It may be likened to a background emission which contributes an influence for a very long time. In particular, the Uranus cycle (84 years) may be likened to an intermittent "hiccup" which interrupts and upsets expected routines.

Cosmic energy vibrates according to cycle frequency because the nature of cosmic body movement is cyclical. Although each natal pattern is a unique vibration and resonates to a particular frequency, cosmic energy is the linking factor and connects all things together. In this way, effects ripple, resonate, and vibrate through the system. The underlying principle is that everything is interdependent and must, therefore, be considered.

Earth Rhythm

Earth rhythms are influenced by cosmic energy cycles.

The motion of the Earth is a rotation about an axis. As the Earth spins and slowly orbits the sun, all things are caught in this rhythm, including the daily cycle of a natal pattern. Each natal pattern has a different experience during its daily cycle.

---

18. See "Suggested Reading," Astrological Timing, Dane Rudhyar , on p. 203.

Cycles of the Day

The spatial pattern of a woman's energy cycle moves through time—connecting, reconnecting, or linking with others. It is very complex, yet beautifully arranged in space.

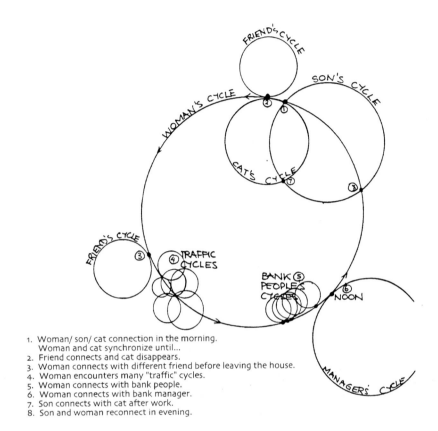

1. Woman/ son/ cat connection in the morning.
   Woman and cat synchronize until...
2. Friend connects and cat disappears.
3. Woman connects with different friend before leaving the house.
4. Woman encounters many "traffic" cycles.
5. Woman connects with bank people.
6. Woman connects with bank manager.
7. Son connects with cat after work.
8. Son and woman reconnect in evening.

This illustration shows a woman's daily cycle, linking with other daily cycles which have been diminished for diagrammatic purposes. The intention is to illustrate the concept of a natal pattern daily cycle by considering only one cycle. In reality, all the cycle paths in the same vicinity would be the same size (once around the Earth) and almost superimposed.

Dots represent sensitive points linked by cosmic energy through alignments. They represent positions where the cycle paths of different natal patterns merge. As the Earth spins, the woman's pattern moves or "cycles" through the day. Encounters occur as her natal pattern cycle intersects the cycles of other natal patterns. The momentary structures of a natal pattern's energy expression during a daily cycle are arrangements of cosmic energy.

Encounter in a Daily Cycle

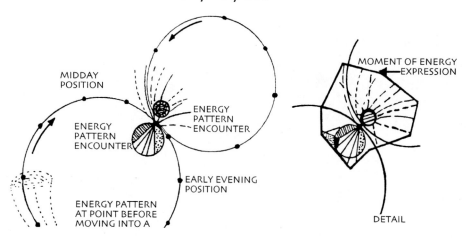

Natal Pattern Movement in a Daily Cycle

This diagram shows in very simple terms the movement of a natal pattern through a day. The pattern is shown at the "beginning" of the day with one of its energy fields. The dots represent the various positions as the pattern moves in the daily cycle. The encounter with another natal pattern occurs at a particular point marked by the moment of energy expression. It is shown in detail as a shape in space, in which particular energy is contained in the moment of its expression.

As the Earth spins on its axis, natal patterns form, connect, disconnect, and disintegrate in the process of cosmic body re-arrangement—the movement of energy in space.[19]

Moments in a Daily Cycle

This diagram shows a few of the moments during a day.
They are represented to demonstrate linking.[20]
The shapes represent moments in space.
The shapes created by moments of energy expression become dimensions[21]

---

19. See "Energy Moves into Space" on page 107.
20. See "Momentary Sequence is an Energy Path" on page 97; p. 95; and "Crystalline Corridor" on page 136.
21. See "Momentary Cosmic Energy Structure Momentary Energy Shape" on page 135.

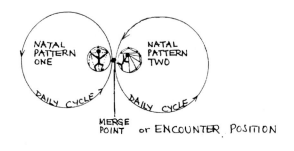

Cosmic Linking

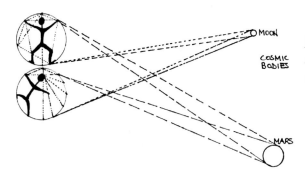

Natal patterns one and two are drawn separately to show details of linking. In reality the energy paths merge during connection.

The Moon in Aspect to Mars is a Global Influence

Natal patterns one and two are drawn together to show cosmic energy linking in both patterns. Internal energy directions, or axes, connect different sensitive points causing individual pattern responses. The effect on Earth depends on these responses. The cosmic energy expression in this moment at the daily cycle merge point is triggered by the moon, Mars, and Earth. For these two patterns the global influence (moon square Mars 90°) triggers a specific response. As the moon moves out of alignment, the shape created by these energy pathways breaks apart. The moment has passed.

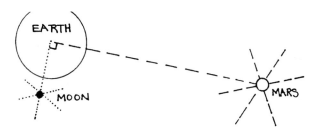

Synchronicity

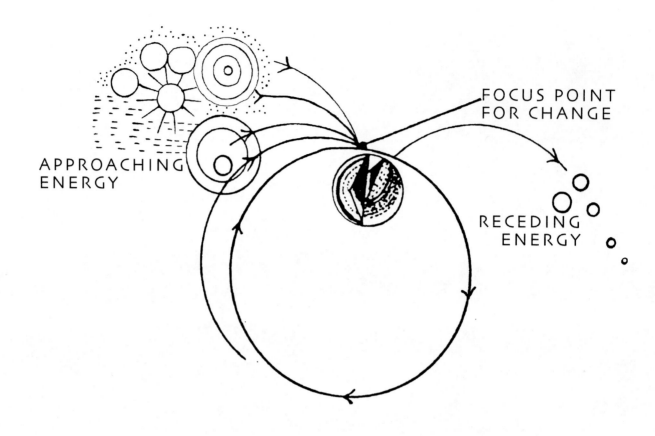

This illustration shows a natal pattern at a point on its cycle. Energy with which the pattern was involved has moved away and is receding. The moments of that energy connection are in the past. Energy with which the pattern will become involved is approaching; those moments are still in the future. The position where the approaching energy will connect with the natal pattern is shown at the focus point. At the time of expression, the moment will be now or the present. Regardless of the amount of energy involved, all moments are significant. The moments when great changes occur for a natal pattern are very meaningful to that pattern. Different natal pattern phases often have their inception at those times. Moments occur through synchronicity because all cosmic energy movement interlocks in the energy grid.

Flow Through Moments
Life Path Directions

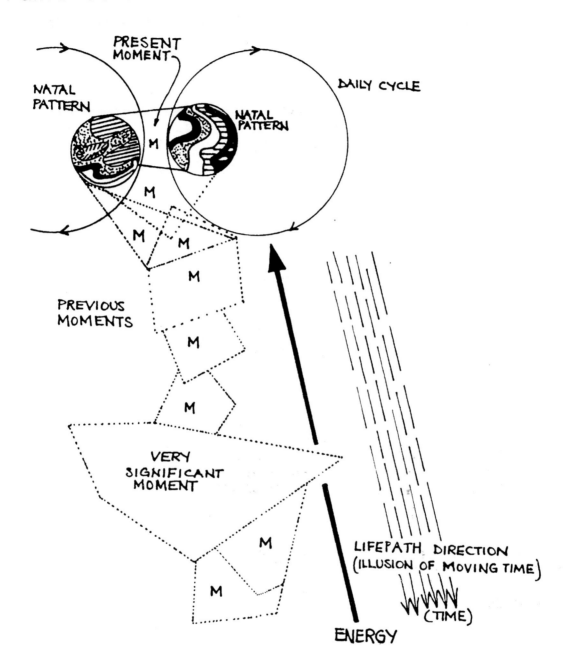

Energy Flow: The Linking of Moments

In this symbolic diagram, in the moment of expression energy exists in a particular shape or form. After expression, another moment occurs as energy expresses itself again and another energy shape forms. Each momentary path is part of the cosmic energy network or circuitry. Energy continues to move, giving the illusion of time passing.

The Linking Force

The diagram on the following page illustrates symbolically the linking force of cosmic energy in a sequence of moments. Each moment is depicted as an angular shape within which a natal pattern (dot) is surrounded by its energy field (circle). The diagram is drawn deliberately to show that each moment corresponds to a particular shape. Each shape describes a particular arrangement and combination of cosmic energy, which forces expression in a specific way.

Each energy expression identifies a moment. Each momentary shape is specific to the response of a natal pattern to prevailing cosmic influences. Each shape is part of a natal pattern energy path. Each path is a different cosmic energy direction on Earth because each natal pattern responds differently. Thus, it is the natal pattern which is the limiting factor in each energy path or destiny.[22]

It should be noted that the angular, or crystalline, forms are indeed momentary. Most of the time energy shapes adopt a curved form, as cosmic energy moves from one moment into the next.[23]

Cosmic links with natal patterns create our moments on Earth. This energy movement through moments is how cosmic energy links all things together and identifies time in an energy continuum.[24]

CONCEPT: The movement of cosmic energy is the linking force in the cosmos.

22. See "Lifepath" on page 184.
23. See "Amorphous Form" on page 98.
24. See "Energy Moves into Space" on page 107.

Momentary Energy Structures

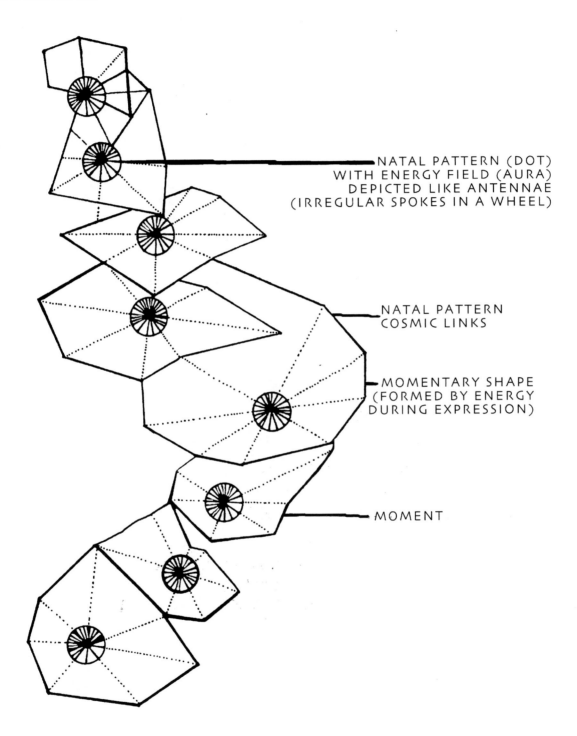

NATAL PATTERN (DOT)
WITH ENERGY FIELD (AURA)
DEPICTED LIKE ANTENNAE
(IRREGULAR SPOKES IN A WHEEL)

NATAL PATTERN
COSMIC LINKS

MOMENTARY SHAPE
(FORMED BY ENERGY
DURING EXPRESSION)

MOMENT

Momentary Sequence is an Energy Path

Momentary Emergence
Faceted Gem Analogy

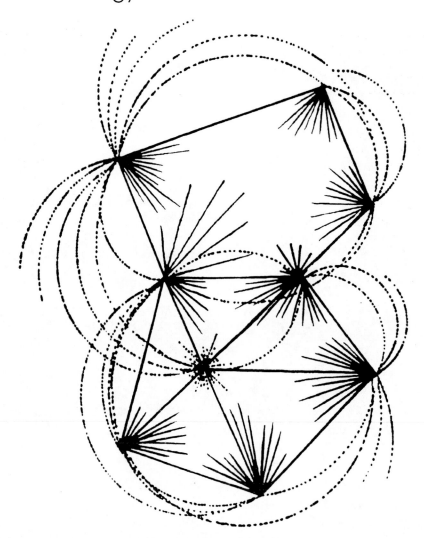

Amorphous Form

Although a moment itself is of a geometric or crystalline nature, cosmic movement pulls cosmic energy fields into non-angular shapes both before and after the moment of energy expression. These shapes are weaker energy fields, which surround the moment itself. They may be likened to non-faceted gems that in their amorphous state exhibit irregular forms.

As one moment links with another, an energy field begins to form in which the prevailing global influences begin to affect specific sensitive points. The geometric shape begins to appear as a raw crystal protrudes from the rough rock. Linking at exact alignment allows the dazzling crystalline shape of each moment to emerge as a faceted gem is revealed from its amorphous form.

Cosmic Energy Grid

Cosmic energy has its effect on Earth at focus points by means of alignments among cosmic bodies. These energy pathways form an angular network of cosmic body emissions, which may be likened to a vast crystalline lattice in which all things exist.

Movement within this unseen energy framework is rather like passing freely through a forest. Not until one bumps into a tree, stumbles over a fallen log, or is brushed by an overhanging branch is one made physically aware of a particular place among the trees. These places in the forest where something happens are analogous to energy focus points on Earth, or merge points within the cosmic energy grid.

A natal pattern draws in cosmic energy according to its sensitive points. In environments where there is little or no interference, the process is simple. In busy environments where there are many natal patterns (focus points) together, there can be a state of energy deprivation. Too many natal patterns are competing in and overloading the space so that there is insufficient energy for all the moments created in the space. In human experience one can feel tired and exhausted, and long to remove oneself from the scene—a downtown department store, a crowded cocktail party, a hectic political meeting.

Picture of Energy

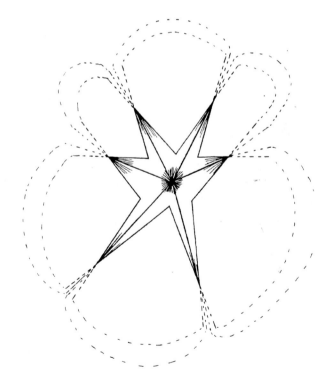

Shapes in Physical Reality Exhibit Curves

Each natal pattern is a focus for incoming cosmic energy which links internal axes through sensitive points. External energy directions form crystalline or geometric shapes around patterns at perfect alignment. Energy fields manifest like the petals of a flower. Energy is thus contained within a specific shape. Shapes in physical reality exhibit curves as the momentary effect lingers in a turning Earth.

Focus

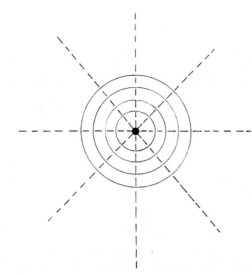

Each Emission is Specific to its Source

Cosmic energy radiates from source points. Radiants become more and more separated as the distance increases. Energy moving towards a focal point behaves conversely. The influence of incoming energy is felt increasingly as the focus point is approached and with maximum effect at perfect alignment.

Shape

Cosmic energy pathways describe geometric shapes.
One of these shapes is the cone.

Without a focus, cosmic energy has little, if any, influence, and is therefore inaccessible, or without significant effect. The cone concentrates energy. As cosmic bodies approach alignment with the Earth, the shape of their emissions forms a cone of energy. These emissions reach maximum concentration and are the most powerful at the point of the cone. They have the greatest influence at this focus point during perfect alignment. The moon plays the most significant role in focusing and, thus, concentrating cosmic energy.

The point of the cone is the focus position where cosmic emissions connect with the Earth. When this position coincides with a sensitive point in a natal pattern there is a cosmic energy interaction. As a cosmic body connection is made with a particular sensitive point in a natal pattern, internal energy axes immediately link other sensitive points within the pattern. This triggers a natal pattern response according to the natal and cosmic influences that are linked. What happens is determined by the way in which the particular combination of energy influences and, therefore, principles are arranged and interact.[25]

---

25. See: "Suggested Reading," *The Combination of Stellar influences*, on p. 203.

The process of alignment with sensitive points (energy terminals on Earth) not only causes unique responses within natal patterns, but also causes natal pattern interaction as it links different patterns and, therefore, energy terminals together. These moments of cosmic energy interaction, observed as events on Earth, are all represented by specific crystalline or geometric shapes. The process may be imagined as constantly changing shapes, in which invisible dynamic crystals occur and fracture and where the turning Earth causes curves in physical reality.

Positions of cosmic energy interaction (expression) are known as merge points. These energy focus points mark positions on natal pattern cycles. Known as cycle markers, merge points identify events on Earth and in the lives of individuals. Humans note these events in terms of past, present, and future and associate them with the passage of time.

CONCEPT: A moment is represented by a crystalline or geometric shape.

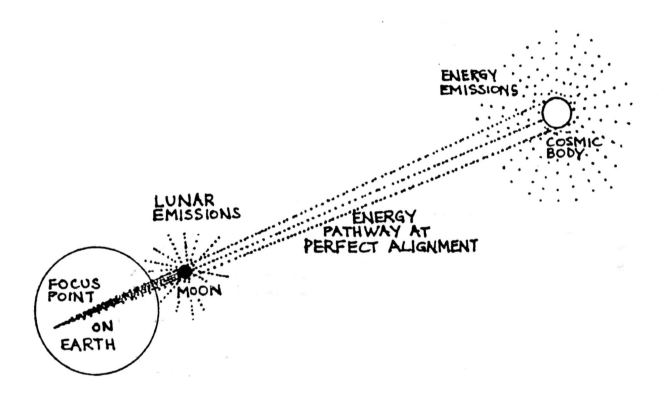

Energy Pathway at Perfect Alignment

The moon plays the most significant role in focusing and, thus, concentrating cosmic energy.

Summary for Part One

1. Nothing happens by chance.
2. Everything which happens is a result of energy expression.
3. All energy expressions are directly related to cosmic influences.
4. Energy is expressed according to pattern interaction.
5. Cosmic energy arrangements form multidimensional energy structures.
6. Cosmic energy causes all things to happen.
7. Natal patterns determine connection.
8. Energy principles determine expression.
9. Energy cycles determine momentary sequence.
10. A moment on Earth is the precursor of the sixth dimension—the invisible shape.
11. A moment is the shape of an energy structure in space.
12. A moment captures the shape of energy expression.
13. A moment exists forever in the sixth dimension. It is a universal record.

THESIS STATEMENT: The natal pattern is an essential energy unit.

CONCEPTS: Cosmic energy is responsible for everything that happens.

Events on Earth are cosmic energy expressions.

Lunar Cycle: During the lunar cycle, the moon aspects each cosmic body in turn. These links occur several times at different angles each month, thus, constantly bringing the cosmos into focus on Earth. Each link contributes a particular influence which is felt around the world. The effect is global. This process not only triggers what happens on Earth, but also continually reinforces the lunar principle—our moods and how we feel.

Response: The response of each natal pattern to the lunar cycle constantly reinforces its individual nature. Different angles of alignment allow different degrees to come into focus, thereby giving different natal patterns a chance to be in the limelight.

Daily Cycle: At the same time, the rotation of the Earth causes each natal pattern to experience the diurnal movement of the Earth. In this book this movement is termed the daily cycle.

Annual Cycle: Every year during the Earth's cycle, the orbit of the Earth causes each natal pattern to pass through the 360° of the zodiac.

Effect: Things happens on Earth when the positions of sensitive points in natal patterns coincide with the energy focus points of cosmic body alignments (energy pathways).

Cycle Merge: Without the phenomenon of cycle merge, the way things are would be more easily recognized. In particular the Uranian cycle, the nature of which is to change and re-arrange things, makes interpretation complex.

Interpretation: Cycle interpretation depends on the arrangement of energy; therefore, the pattern is essential. The energy pattern which is responsible for individual uniqueness causes each of us to respond uniquely to energy principles.

Uniqueness: Uniqueness is, thus, a camouflage for cycle interpretation. Nevertheless, energy cycles exist in simple and complex form bringing energy into alignment at the focus points of cyclical merging.

Eight • Time

Furneux Pelham Church Clock

When as a child I laughed and wept,
Time crept:
When as a youth I dreamed and talked
Time walked.
When I became a full-grown man.
Time ran:
As older still I daily grew,
Time flew;
Soon shall I find in travelling on,
Time gone.

Perspective

It is first essential to reconsider the concept of time and, as we begin to comprehend, perchance our attitude towards time will change.

In the modern world, time describes several things.

There is time "how long," a period in which events occur. It is the duration of a marriage, a manicure, a meeting, a period of fame, or loneliness. In this context the cosmic interpretation is the moment which encompasses the energy expression, as in a tooth extraction, a wedding ceremony, a lifetime.

There is time "when," a specific time in daily affairs for appointments, work schedules, or newscasts. In this context time is an energy focus point in space, a position relative to all else in the cosmos. It has to do with cosmic body alignments which involve timing or synchronized rhythms. Time "when" is linked to cycles which contain destiny and karma.

There is time "passing," where time is considered to be a moving phenomenon, and which, once passed, never returns. Time passing is an illusion and reflects a general misconception of time.

There is an old saying that "time waits for no man," which implies that time is moving. The popular phrase, "time goes by," reflects and perpetuates what seems to happen from a human perspective. Events happen in sequence so that, to most individuals, the concept of time is of something which passes. Time does not pass. It is the individual who passes. It is energy which passes as it moves into space. In reality, energy rearranges itself, pegging time in the process so that there is an illusion of time passing. The analogy is of a person who is looking from the window of a moving train—the scenery appears to be moving past. However, the individual is moving through the scenery with the train; the individual experiences relative motion.[1]

Today is different from yesterday. The Earth has been turning. Everything has moved into a different position relative to where it was yesterday. Cosmic energy has rearranged itself. The individual experiences this movement as the passage of time, but this is inaccurate; the individual has merely moved into another space.

Cosmic bodies represent energy sources in motion. As these bodies move, cosmic energy re-arranges itself and links sensitive points among natal patterns with the cosmos. What happens identifies the moment: a standing ovation, a burst pipe, the ring of a door bell. On Earth this process is known as time. It is the relationship between cosmic energy and space.

CONCEPT: Time does not pass: energy moves in space.

Time is an energy phenomenon.

---

1. See "Energy Flow: The Linking of Moments" on page 95.

Concept

Time is a non-physical dimension.

Time is the shape in which everything exists—the momentary shape created as cosmic energy expresses itself, a dimension imprinted with energy which identifies it like a template. It is the shape in which something occurs. Time is an energy-defined space. Without energy, time is unidentified and space is void. Cosmic energy brings time into existence. Position is important, since each moment occurs at a cycle merge point—the position where sensitive points in natal patterns align with cosmic energy pathways during the daily cycle (the Earth's daily rotation). In this way a dimension is a marker, like a colored ribbon on a trail, or a buoy at sea. It is how cosmic energy links moments on Earth with cosmic configurations and pinpoints time.[2]

As length, breadth, and height define a shape in physical reality, time describes the fourth, fifth, and sixth dimensions in non-physical reality.

4D   Time "how long" is the fourth dimension.
It corresponds to the duration of the moment.

5D   Time "when" is the fifth dimension.
It corresponds to the relative position in space.

6D   Time "what happens" is the sixth dimension.
It corresponds to the energy expression itself.
The sixth dimension is accurate because there
is only one way that cosmic energy expresses
itself in each natal pattern interaction.[3]

In the present moment, or now, 4D, 5D, and 6D are one.

CONCEPT: All dimensions are created by energy, including those of time.

2. See "Cube Example" on page 125.
3. See "The Dinner Party Shape" on page 132.

Energy Moves into Space

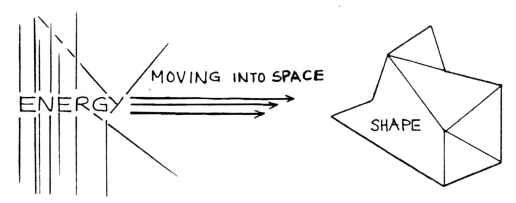

Energy moves into space to form the
shape in which it will express itself.

Each shape in space corresponds
to the shape of a particular moment.
Each momentary shape is a dimension
in which particular cosmic influences
express themselves.

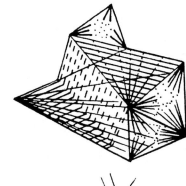

Energy fixes time in space. It defines a shape
and moves on. The shape continues to exist as an
energy sensitive space: a dimension in time.
Access is only through an energy code.

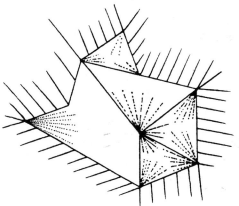

Without Energy Time Does Not Exist and Space is Void

Time Frame

Energy expression identifies time.

Sharing a moment is being in the same energy shape. Being in the same time frame is equivalent to being in the same cyclical interval.[4] "In the weeks that followed" refers to a dimension or time frame descriptive of a particular period. "From this point in time" refers to a particular moment in a time frame—the moment when something important happened. In terms of cosmic energy, each moment is linked to a position of energy expression that marks specific cosmic activity. In this way, cosmic energy pinpoints time.

Ski-Lift Analogy

As skiers unload from a ski lift, a person observing at the unloading ramp is aware of a constant flow of skiers—approaching unseen, appearing, unloading, and skiing away to disappear. Their apparent disappearance is an illusion (Neptune) for they are still somewhere on the mountain; the skiers are in another space; a different position, another dimension.

The skiers continue to arrive until the lift closes. For the person observing the unloading ramp, that portion of the day corresponds to moments on a cycle in which many others shared a few brief minutes. The moments are now in another dimension. The preceding days were similar and represent different dimensions with enough similarity for energy overlay to distort distinct memory recall.[5] For the person at the ramp, it will be remembered as a period of watching skiers unload where the days all merge in the past. Nevertheless, in terms of physics, the dimensions are separate and occurred in sequence. Sequence is merely the order of events due to energy expression (skiers unloading). It is not the movement of time, but of energy.

This analogy illustrates energy repetition in daily cycles which is marked as a way of life for a period (time frame) for the person observing the ramp. Only very significant energy arrangements allow one day to distinguish itself from another, such as an accident or lift malfunction.

---

4. See "The Shared Moment" on page 131.
5. See "Overlay or Superimposition" on page 86.

Similar Daily Cycles:

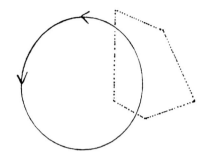

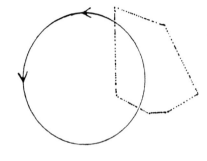

DIMENSION OVERLAY

In the illustration each circle represents a
natal pattern daily cycle. The circles
represent five consecutive days. Each
angular shape represents a moment: a
portion of the day. The moments represent
daily events: routines which occur during
work schedules and in ordinary, everyday
living. The moments are therefore very
similar, so that the days do not easily
distinguish themselves in the human mind.
Although each shape represents a different
dimension, when the circles are linked in a
spiral to form the natal pattern path, the
dimensions are subjected to overlay
because the individual natal pattern passes
through almost the same circular space
from day to day as the earth turns. Only a
very significant energy expression creates a
dimension which is so different that it is
noticed. Events in the daily cycle depend
on cosmic interaction with each natal
pattern so that each daily cycle is a portion
of an individual energy path: it is the way
energy moves through space. In human
terms each portion is part of the life cycle
(lifetime). For most of us consecutive daily
cycles are similar because the prevailing
cosmic configuration is similar and changes
slowly. For most of us for considerable
periods the cosmic configuration is not
disrupting our lives.

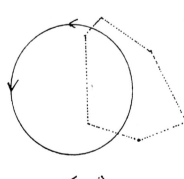

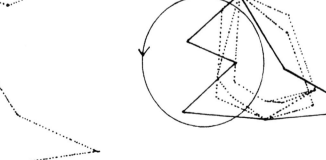

Containment Concept

Minutes/Moments

Time contains all things.

Energy cycles envelop, or wrap around, moments, thus containing many expressions of energy within particular periods. The phenomenon manifests as phases, or periods, in life and, on another scale, as epochs. An enveloping cycle is observed in the life cycle of the flowering bulb—the various moments of leaf appearance, budding, flowering and withering are all contained in the larger, longer moment of the entire bulb cycle.[6] Thus, time encapsulates energy; it is the dimension in which cosmic energy imprints itself forever.

In terms of physics, everything exists within something larger or greater than itself. Thus, energy cycles extend moments. Each moment extends beyond a single moment, through the linking nature of cosmic energy. Although an original moment may have lasted for sixty minutes, when the dimension of that moment is accessed, the minutes are no longer a measure. This occurs in the moment of memory recall: the flash of a scene past, where the moment embodies the entire event in a fraction of a second. The moment is immediate (Uranus).[7] When this happens, time as we understand it on Earth is collapsed like a telescope and illustrates that the nature of time is dependent on cosmic energy.

On our familiar time scale, a minute is a measure, a specific distance in circular or arc-time. All minutes are equal. Minutes do not pass; days, hours, and minutes mark energy positions in space. Moments are unequal. Moments pass because moments are energy structures, shapes in space determined by energy expression. The moments in our lives all occur within energy cycles or arc-time.[8]

The momentary nature of time is actually the changing arrangement of cosmic energy.

Moments pass; minutes mark time.

Moments are invisible energy shapes in space.

CONCEPT: A moment is a shape in space.

6. See "Within this flux, all things exist;" on page 73.
7. See "Uranus forces energy patterns to evolve." on page 63.
8. See "Cyclical Phenomena" on page 77.

Jet Lag

Exciting events appear to make time go faster, but it is really an elaborate energy arrangement. When a lot of energy is in space, there is much activity, a lot happens. Excitement occupies the senses; time appears to fly and is mostly unnoticed. When energy is restricted, the day seems to drag.[9] People watch the clock. Humans sense the difference and attribute it to the passage of time. It is actually the passage of energy. Since we are natal patterns ourselves, we are part of the motion. Other energy movement is relative to ours.[10] Although everything is moving, to the human observer a cat springs through a doorway; the doorway does not move. A car speeds on the highway; the highway does not pass, like a conveyer belt beneath the car. A person walks into a room. The room does not pass by the person, but remains for others to enter and leave. Eventually the room disappears when the building is demolished. The residual space allows something else to be built and different energy to move in.

Having evolved through millions of years at the Earth's rotational rate, humans find it difficult adjusting to jet lag. When flying from west to east, cosmic body alignments to sensitive points happen more quickly than usual. Links among cosmic bodies, particularly lunar links, are also encountered more rapidly due to the shorter interval or time frame. The individual cannot cope with the speed of the changing energy arrangements. In reverse, when flying from east to west, time seems to drag. Two o'clock in the afternoon seems to linger forever because alignments happen more slowly and last longer. The afternoon stretches itself. One feels tired and drained of energy as if there were not enough.

Different cyclical intervals prevent everything from happening at once, so that moments occur in sequence. The individual is aware of something which passes and mistakenly labels it time. When there seems not to be enough time for anything, it means energy expressed itself in a way that did not allow certain things to be done. In reality, different energy expressed itself than was expected.

9. See "Saturn delays." on page 61.
10. See "Cycles of the Day" on page 91; and "5D" on page 124.

Nine • Space

Concept

"Space and time, matter and energy become a completely self-contained package."

Michael White and John Gribbin
Reader's Digest, February 1993
A Brief History of Stephen Hawking

Time is the cosmic relationship between energy and space.

Space is the environment in which energy expresses itself. It is outer space: the little known, extensive void which separates cosmic bodies; it is inner space which separates atoms within molecules; it is indoor living space, pipeline interiors, and the outdoor environment.

There is a cosmic relationship between energy and space. The movement of cosmic bodies represents energy sources in motion where orbits are like circular tracks in space. As cosmic bodies move and energy rearranges itself, alignments trigger responses in natal patterns and cause moments on Earth. Interaction among natal patterns links energy expression with position. The process identifies this connection and brings time into existence. Since each moment occurs in a specific position on each natal pattern daily cycle, moments pinpoint energy focus points within the cycles of cosmic bodies. Each event is a marker on a cycle—the outward manifestation of an energy interaction in physical reality. Within this context, space "waits" for energy to link it with time.

In physical form, a cube is a three-dimensional shape in space. In non-physical form, it is a three-dimensional space, like a hollow cube; it is a space contained within a shape. When the cube in physical form moves in space, or when energy in non-physical form moves into the cube shape, time is brought into existence. Thus, space remains undefined unless associated with energy.

Undefined space has no dimension. There is no shape. Time does not exist.

Specificity

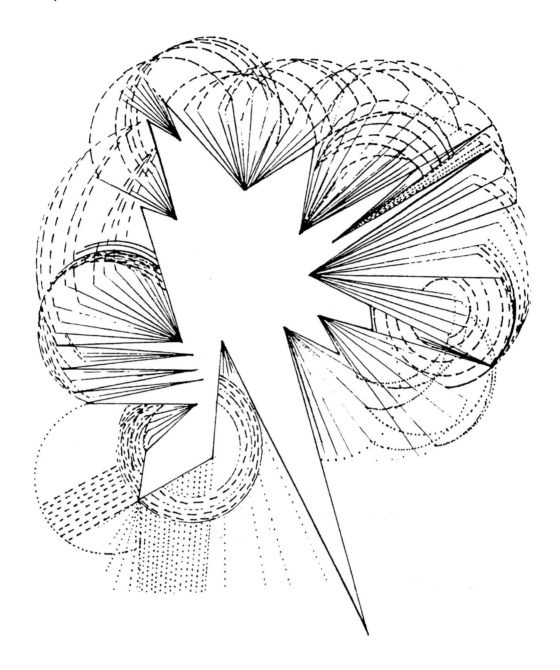

Each Energy Expression is Associated with a Particular Shape

In this illustration, the space represents a special shape which only a particular energy structure will fit. If an energy structure does not fit a shape, the corresponding expression will not occur. Cosmic energy will create a different shape in its expression. A different moment will occur.

Ten • Shape

Shape Definition

Cosmic energy defines shapes in space.

When space is defined in the moment of energy expression, it becomes a shape which corresponds to a cosmic energy structure. The shape is specific to the expression where each expression of energy is a particular moment in the cosmos. These momentary structures remain as energy sensitive shapes, or dimensions of time. Without energy shape does not exist.

Natal patterns are cosmic energy structures which exist like occupants of particular spaces. Formed during the moment of birth, each natal pattern shape is created by energy directions among sensitive points. Internal connections among these focal points are energy axes within the structure which force the natal pattern to behave in a particular way that directs energy movement on Earth. External energy directions, or cosmic links, create fluctuating shapes which form the energy environment, or energy field, within which natal patterns exist. The shape of these energy fields changes as energy directions rearrange themselves. For this reason the effect of cosmic energy is linked to its structural nature.

Shapes must share both space and energy. The shapes that energy alignments form create the constantly changing shapes which jostle for space and compete for available energy. Misfit among shapes may cause humans to experience uncomfortable feelings.

Saturn involves disciplined structure, shapes that do not yield and can therefore, block or restrict energy movement. When Saturn is in a position of influence, cosmic energy is limited. Too little energy creates an unfulfilled need leading to restriction. Shapes are forced to diminish or separate.[1] Humans may feel isolated and lacking in energy.

---

1. See "Saturn creates the feeling of loneliness." on page 62.

The Importance of Shape:

Natal Patterns Always Identify with a Specific Shape

Cosmic energy constantly bombards natal patterns.

The energy field which surrounds the human body is part of the individual's space. The shape of this energy field changes constantly because it is dependent on cosmic links. When cosmic links intensify, individuals become "locked within a structure" which others cannot penetrate. This may be a natal feature or occur for the duration of an energy transit.[2]

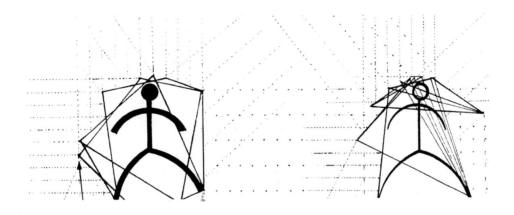

Everything Exists in an Energy Shape
This illustration is symbolic of existence within a shape.

---

2. See Transit, Glossary, p. 212.

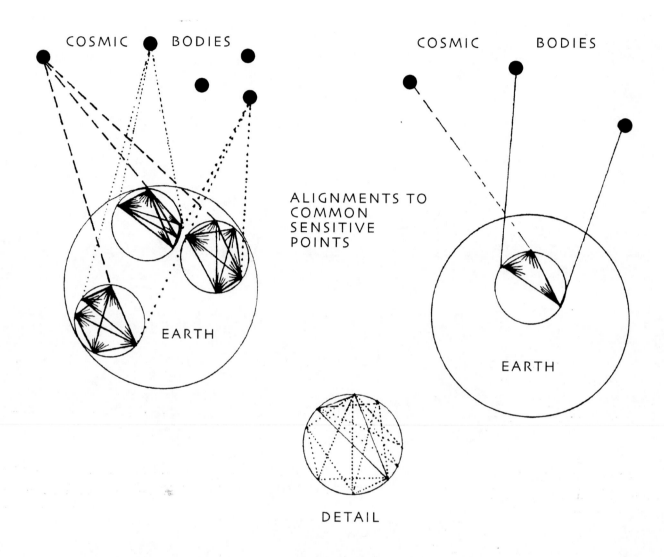

COSMIC BODIES

COSMIC BODIES

ALIGNMENTS TO
COMMON
SENSITIVE
POINTS

EARTH

EARTH

DETAIL

Natal Patterns are Like Invisible Crystals

The above illustration shows three natal patterns linked to the cosmos and a momentary shape as they interact.[3]

3. See "Crystalline Concept" on page 20.

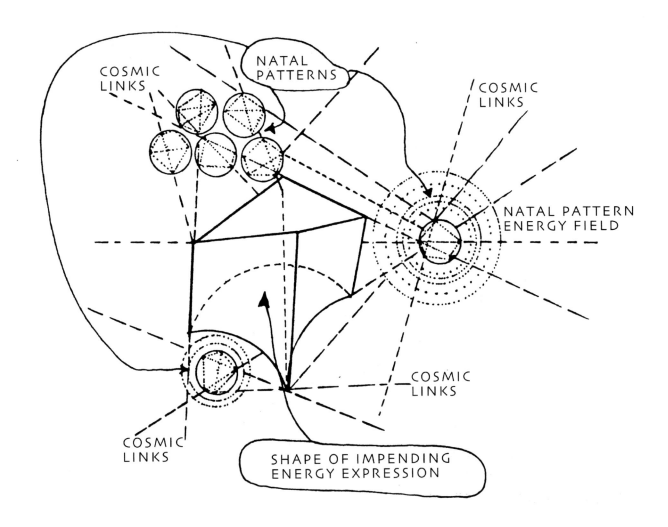

COSMIC LINKS

NATAL PATTERNS

COSMIC LINKS

NATAL PATTERN ENERGY FIELD

COSMIC LINKS

COSMIC LINKS

SHAPE OF IMPENDING ENERGY EXPRESSION

An Impending Moment of Energy Expression

This shows natal patterns preparing to enter a space-shape where cosmic links will cause natal-pattern interaction. The illustration is simplified and presented artistically in an attempt to show the complexity of the energy arrangement that exists prior to the moment of energy expression.

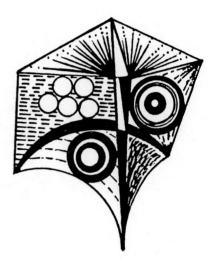

Shape is an Integral Part of Cosmic Energy Expression

Natal patterns are units of shape. Within any moment, all the separate patterns become one energy structure which fits the shape of energy expression. The shape is the dimension of its occurrence. This is the underlying principle of the cosmic energy system. There is only one space which is filled by many patterns, all arranged according to the laws of cosmic energy and space. It is a principle of unit, where one is composed of many and each is complete in itself.

In the cyclical continuum of cosmic energy, shapes form and break apart. New shapes come into existence.[4]

Energy Fits the Shape

This illustration is drawn in circular form to emphasize that energy fits the shape during expression. The strongly circular shape contains the forces during the moment, and may be likened to a controlled reaction chamber. In the moment of energy expression, there is one shape within which all the individual patterns connect. The shape is the space of occurrence. It is symbolic of cosmic energy within an activity zone.[5]

---

4. See "Momentary Sequence is an Energy Path" on page 97.
5. See "Energy Fits the Shape" on page 46.

Shape is defined space.

A rigid steel pipeline or flexible rubber hose are both tubular structures: cylindrical spaces with restrictive outer coverings. The shape forces or directs inner energy movements in either of two directions. A change in shape causes different movement. A change in energy causes the shape to change. It may buckle, twist, or explode. In the same way, energy structures fit a shape during expression. Whatever the shape, energy components completely fill the space. As orbital motion causes the prevailing or global configuration to rearrange itself, energy links with sensitive points are forced to break apart because the angular directions change. The shape changes and the moment passes. This releases the natal pattern for reconnection, which causes different shapes to form.

"With her foot on the threshold she waited a moment longer in a scene which was vanishing even as she looked, and then, as she moved and took Minta's arm and left the room, it changed, it shaped itself differently; it had become, she knew, giving one last look at it over her shoulder, already the past."

Virginia Woolf
To the Lighthouse

"…it shaped itself differently…" refers to a rearrangement of energy.

What makes it happen is a force, a specific cosmic energy influence. The way it happens is an astro-physical interaction. The process is a cosmic energy relationship among different natal patterns, all of which respond uniquely to the same cosmic influences. The result is a rearrangement of energy; a different structural configuration, or shape, is created in space. The effect on Earth through natal-pattern interaction is observed as an event—waiting in a scene before leaving the room on Minta's arm.

Spatial arrangement determines energy structures. This means that configuration allows momentary energy shapes to pass through energy shapes without connection. In theory connection is possible with more patterns than actually occurs. However, connection does not happen with all things, because energy cycles in configuration. Cycles prevent an entangled mass.[6]

---

6. See "Cosmic Orchestra" on page 23.

Principle of Energy Passage

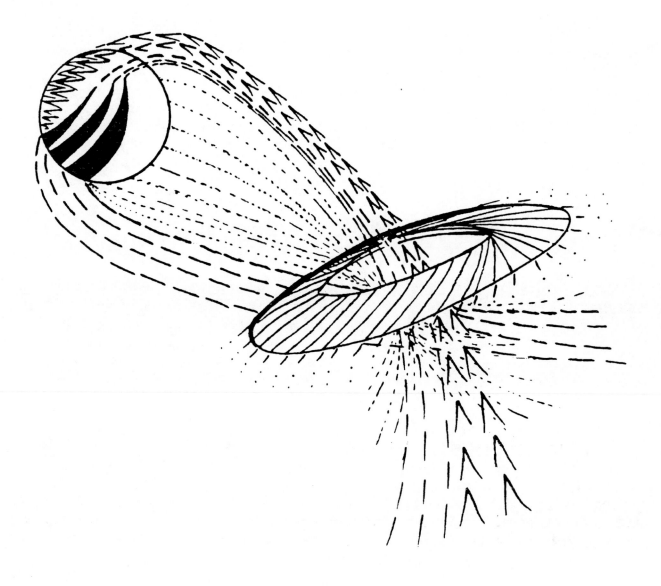

This symbolic illustration shows an energy shape passing through an energy shape. Neither energy field affects the other. Both shapes remain intact because there is no connection.

Picture of Energy

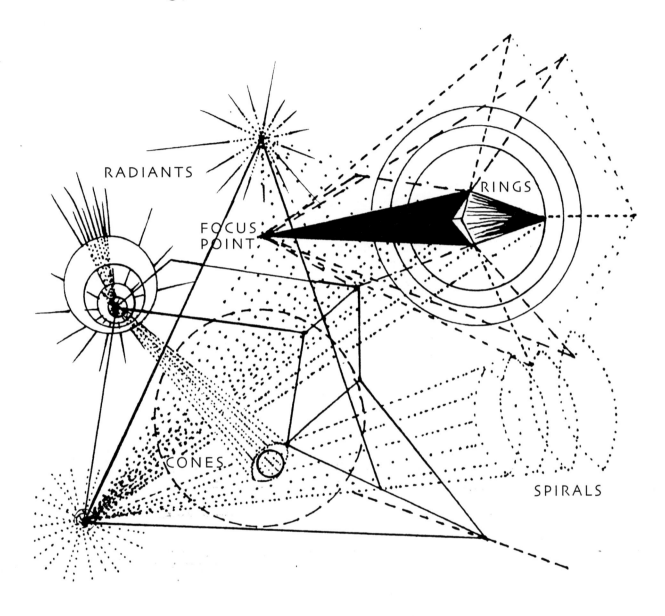

Cosmic energy patterns are energy arrangements which exist as structures or shapes in space. They are multidimensional since everything is linked with cycles.

This symbolic illustration shows the penetration of one energy structure by another. Energy centers (focus points), energy radiants, energy cones, energy rings, and the beginning of energy spirals are shown to illustrate the complexity of cosmic energy fields, movement and influences.

Cosmic energy depends on arrangement; it involves shape.

Cosmic energy is transmitted by means of alignments among cosmic bodies (energy sources) and natal patterns (energy codes or terminals) on Earth. These energy pathways form intricate geometrical structures like crystalline axes that act like energy co-ordinates. When several terminals and sources are linked, energy can be either dissipated and have less impact, or so concentrated by focus that the impact is extremely intensified. The effect passes as alignments change.

Unlike energy from a single source, such as the heat from a fire, cosmic energy originates from multiple sources and arrives on Earth from different angular directions. For this reason, cosmic energy influences are complex. The effect is always due to a combination of energy emissions which have an influence according to their arrangement, namely the structure, or network of alignments.

CONCEPT: Cosmic energy processes are associated with shape—the configuration of alignments.

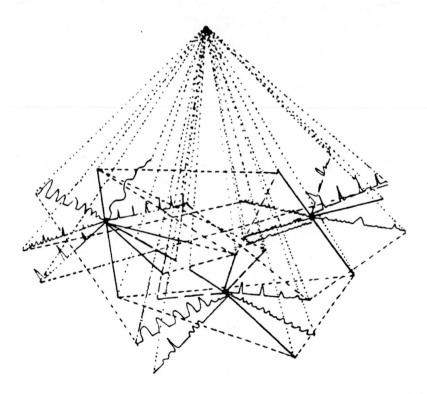

The Process of Transmission is Essentially Concerned with Shape[7]

---

7. See "A Momentary Cosmic Energy Shape" on page 2.

City Scene

The cosmos is reflected in the shape of all things on Earth.

City buildings reach skywards
creating shapes and spaces
as ice crystals erupt
and protrude from the Earth.

Each time a city reaches up: skyscrapers,
                                  minarets, steeples, television towers;
             down: subways
                                  basements, underground parking, sewers;
                out: suburbia
                                  access routes, railways, urban sprawl…

Each city reaches into space and creates its own shape.
Each city reflects the cosmos in its moment on Earth.

Throughout history cities have emerged and disappeared;
Their shapes reminiscent of prevailing energy influences;
Their life spans determined by their natal patterns.

At the time of writing in the downtown area of Vancouver, the buildings portray an era of architectural towers. In their present form, the collective mass of these beautiful structures exhibit shapes and spaces reminiscent of crystalline forms. Millions of images from reflecting surfaces, and lights from within, augment an unwritten acknowledgment of the crystalline nature of the cosmos.

Eleven • The Invisible Shape

Perspective

A dimension is a facet of time.

We are familiar with three-dimensional shapes found in physical reality. However, invisible multi-dimensional shapes exist within the vastness of the cosmos. These shapes are linked to energy cycles and may be thought of as time frames—space-shapes in which energy memories are stored and interlinked by cosmic energy.

Dimensions are created through energy expression. The first, second, and third dimensions are concerned with space and define shape. The fourth, fifth, and sixth dimensions are cycle linked; they define time.

1D	The first dimension is a focus point:	a position in space, like a source from where cosmic energy emanates, or a position to which it is focused.
2D	The second dimension is an outline:	the lineal definition caused by the links between various points within one plane.
3D	The third dimension is a structure:	a three-dimensional object formed by the links between three or more points not in the same plane (a plane with thickness).
4D	The fourth dimension is an interval:	the duration required for what happens or, in cosmic terms, energy expression.
5D	The fifth dimension is a position:	relative to all else (while children were at school in 1941, soldiers were fighting in World War II; as one person walks along a beach, another reads a book in an aircraft).
6D	The sixth dimension is an energy imprint:	the code for what happens and is accurate. It may be past, present, or future, depending on perspective. As a moment occurs, the fourth, fifth, and sixth dimensions coexist in the present.

The dimension of an energy shape is specific to the expression that forms it. In this way, an energy shape identifies a particular cosmic configuration and natal pattern interaction, or a particular moment in the universe. Without energy, space and time are undefined. Energy links them together in the moment of energy expression, creating a shape in space. Different dimensions are known to humans as time.

Thus, time does not pass. Time is marked by expression as energy moves in space.

CONCEPT: A moment remains in the sixth dimension in energy form.
METAPHYSICAL CONCEPT: A moment exists forever.

The moment of energy expression is a specific cosmic energy shape. It is retained in code form in the sixth dimension as an invisible energy shape.

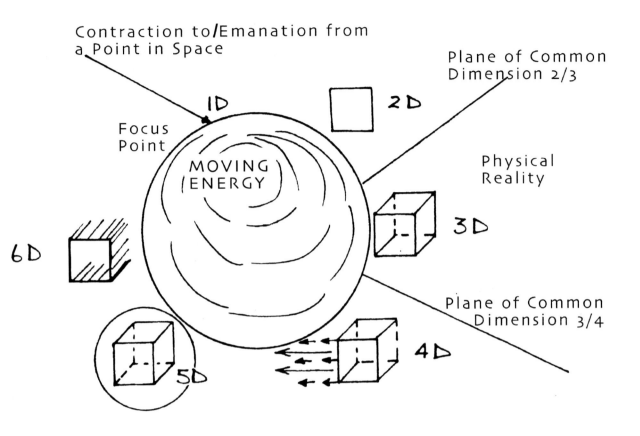

Cube Example

1D	first dimension	focus point (source or target)
2D	second dimension	outline/surface/(rectangle, triangle, circle)
3D	third dimension	structure (plane with thickness, cube, sphere, cylinder)
4D	fourth dimension	interval (time frame, duration of energy expression, movement of cube)
5D	fifth dimension	relative position or location (when, where)
6D	sixth dimension	energy imprint/code for the moment of expression (accurate memory)

456D are one in the moment of energy expression—now.

1D   energy focus point

2D   image of person

3D   human form
      in physical reality

4D   human form in motion:
      duration of activity

5D   position of person
      in motion

6D   energy imprint of moment

Energy Sensitive Shapes in Space

MOMENT:
shape in space defined by energy expression

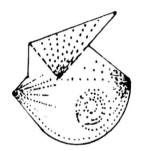

DIMENSION:
shape in space imprinted by energy expression

Dimensions Occupy Positions in Space

In this diagram each dimension is drawn separately to illustrate that each shape is specific to a moment of energy expression. However, dimensions are not only adjacent, but interlocking and superimposed. Only specific energy arrangements detect their existence.

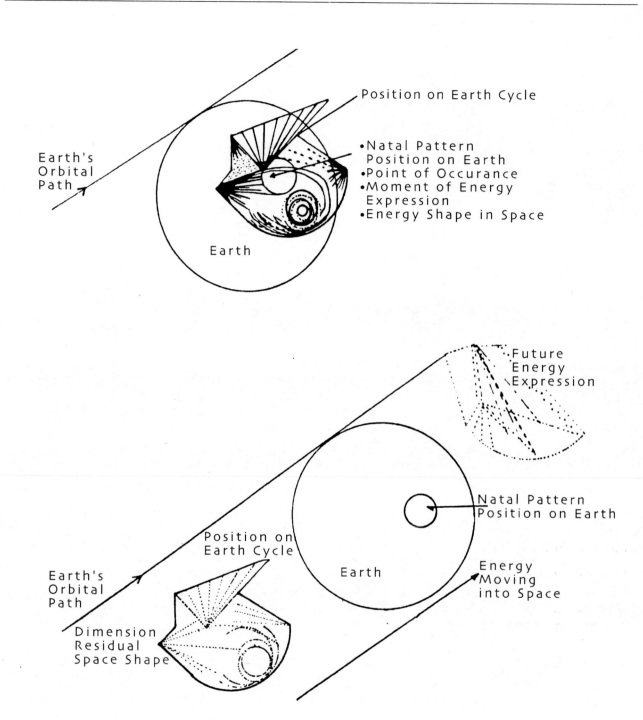

An Imprint or Memory Remains

This illustration shows a natal pattern moving with the Earth and a moment of energy expression. Each moment remains as an energy sensitive shape—an imprint, like a residual code.

Moment of Existence

Each moment is an expression of energy.

From the instant energy response causing an explosion, to the enduring response of mountains to environmental and cosmic bombardment, the energy process is the same. It is always an interaction between cosmic energy and natal patterns—an expression in which a momentary cosmic energy structure occurs. Exactly what happens when this momentary shape occurs is determined by the combination of energy influences. These depend on energy cycles. The moment of its existence is observed in the manifestation of a person during a lifetime; the physical existence of mountains during millennia; or simply an encounter with another person while shopping. A person's lifetime is like an extensive moment in the shape of a time frame, a dimension within which all the person's activities are contained as different momentary shapes that are retained as energy imprints.[1]

The moment of a mountain includes all the physical changes which occur as the mountain is gradually worn away until it no longer exists as a mountain in physical reality.

Everything is in separate dimensions.

Everything exists in an energy shape. When alignments change, the shape breaks apart and the moment is gone.

For all of us, in the moment of reality we exist in an energy shape. We are contained in that moment in a shape which encloses us and excludes others.[2] As the cosmos changes, changing alignments form new shapes. The shape of the moment changes, allowing us to leave or allowing other things to enter a particular space. A residual code remains. Another dimension lingers; another moment begins.[3]

In our moment of existence, we are each in a position on Earth which, at all times, is exactly right for us. We occupy a space, a momentary cosmic shape where energy expresses itself and manifests according to a natal pattern uniquely ours. When I am in my moment and you are in yours, we are in separate moments of existence and, therefore, in separate dimensions. Since we are each in a unique lifetime which intermittently connects with the lifetimes of others, individuals are separated by dimensions. We are energy apart, not distance. It may be observed in a small village where some people never see each other, and in a hospital where patients never meet. Persons in either group are not very distant from each other in space, but the natal patterns, which determine their individual responses and therefore define their respective dimensions, do not permit connection.[4]

The moment of existence is the dimension in which we live. It includes the moment of physical reality and a connection with the past and future through links with other dimensions.

CONCEPT: Co-existent moments are separated by energy, not distance.

---

1. See "Lifetime" on page 169.
2. See "Everything Exists in an Energy Shape" on page 115.
3. See "The Ghosts of Destiny" on page 199.
4. See "Sensitive Points" on page 24.

Concept

The individual relates to dimension as follows:

I am aware of myself, of my surroundings, and of my position within the daily cycle and on any of several cycles.

I am in a particular moment of my existence.

I am able to project my mind or focus on other moments not always my own.

When you are experiencing a moment of existence particular to you, I relate as follows. If I wish to experience that moment, I have to be in it with you (concurrent energy expression: walking through the doorway together). If I wish to reach that moment with you, but am not physically present, I have to access that dimension while you walk through the door. To reach that moment, I have to focus energy. The moment may have passed, is now, or is to arrive. I have to locate it, which is an energy process, and connect with your momentary expression within your space where you exist now. In this process I must reach the sixth dimension. Within this energy context, I will walk through the door with you.

You will have a different experience. You may, and probably will, sense a presence, as if you are not alone. You may suddenly wish I were walking through the doorway with you. I may enter your mind. You may sense, or know, that I am thinking about you, that I am very close. It is your moment of existence which I share through the sixth dimension.

True sharing is in the moment of existence. Only if we share the same moment, do we share the same dimension. We exist together when it is "now" for both of us.

The Shared Moment

An occasion is an energy expression in physical reality.

When five people have dinner together, all share the moment and the memory. All share an energy shape, a dimension.

As prevailing cosmic energy connects with each natal pattern and determines interaction among five people, a moment is created which exists as a dinner party. It leaves a dimension exclusive to the moment. In cosmic terms, the dinner party is an energy shape which is shared by five people. Each of the five natal patterns occupies a position in that shape. Each imprints the dimension individually and collectively. Everything is recorded in energy. When the dinner party is remembered, individual memories are like a replay. A film would show a form of the moment in two-dimensional images. Each of the five persons can access the moment directly through memory and, in theory, experience an exact replay. Others can access the dimension if they can link with the code. None can participate again because that moment has passed forever.

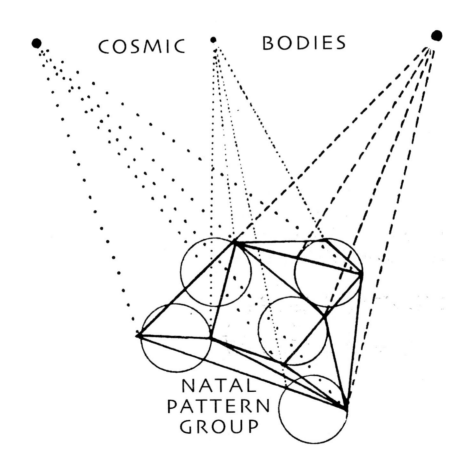

COSMIC BODIES

NATAL PATTERN GROUP

In this illustration (symbolic of the dinner party shape), the circles represent five natal patterns which connect with each other at sensitive points.[5] Straight lines are energy directions which link the patterns. Dotted lines are cosmic links which allow the shape and, therefore, the moment. For diagrammatic purposes only a few connections are shown.

5. See: "Circular Association" on page 22, and diagrams on pages 25, 26, and 31.

The Dinner Party Shape

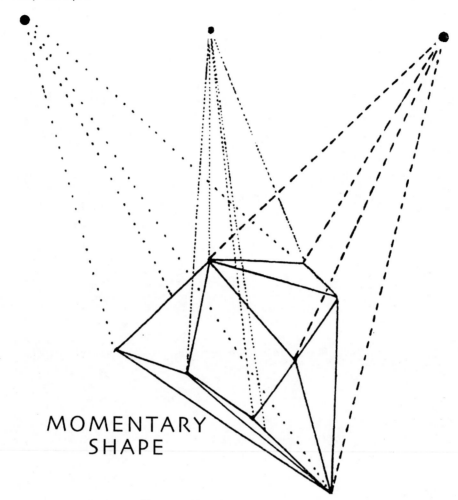

MOMENTARY
SHAPE

The Second Dimension

The effect of Neptune is acknowledged in the second dimension.

The second dimension is an outline, the lineal definition caused by the links between one point and others in the same plane. It is the dimension of images. It is in the realm of Neptune which allows us to see something in non-physical reality: only the image exists, not the reality.

Television is a way of looking into, or seeing, another dimension. Consider a man sitting in a studio. A television camera captures images of the man, who is smiling and talking in animated excitement. The man is in three-dimensional (3D) form in physical reality in his own moment of existence. At the present time he is in the studio. He is in one place.

Through the conversion processes of the television camera and network, images of the man appear on screens throughout the area of transmission. Suddenly his image is everywhere. The man is seen in 2D form by viewers. Yet he is not two dimensional, nor is he in the monitor. The 3D man is an expression of cosmic energy in space, a natal pattern in the moment of its own reality (4D, 5D, 6D). The 2D images are a dimension of his existence and may be recovered for portrayal by various means, such as delayed telecasting, video recording, or photographs. In theory, in 2D form the televised man may exist forever. During the original live telecasting, the 3D man's image was converted to a scrambled energy form (a code), able to pass through a focus point 1D. Throughout the original telecasting, the man's 3D shape was moving into space with the Earth 4D. For every second in time (4D), he simultaneously existed in 5D and 6D.

In human terms the man experiences being in the studio, the moment itself. Viewers experience a dimension of the man.[6]

The Sixth Dimension

Memory is in the sixth dimension.

The sixth dimension is an invisible energy-sensitive shape which lingers in space like a ghost—a spectre which remains as an unseen presence, a structure that is recognized by particular energy arrangements.

Neon Light Analogy

The sixth dimension (6D) may be likened to a neon light; its shape is always there.

Like neon lights which are brightly illuminated at night yet remain dull, colorless forms in the daylight, invisible energy sensitive shapes remain in the cosmos. As cosmic energy connection to these shapes is made, the link activates expression in a particular way just as electrical energy gives light to neon tubes.

If cosmic energy processes could be frozen in time and observed, numerous shapes created by energy directions would appear, forming a vast array of energy structures and links with other dimensions. If this frozen picture were then set in motion, present moments of energy expression would continually form in a kaleidoscope of changing shapes. Intermittently a moment occurs whose shape fits a dimension perfectly. When this happens, a moment reoccurs just as a neon shape lights up again when stimulated by a compatible electrical source. History repeats itself.

The sixth dimension is created in the moment of energy expression. It is formed through the interaction of connecting energy principles and captures a cosmic energy shape which is imprinted with energy specific to the expression, a code which corresponds to the energy structure of a particular moment on Earth. In this way each moment is registered or "fixed" in time, and becomes part of the universal memory. Each moment is different for every natal pattern.

The sixth dimension is accurate.

A moment is accurate. It is what happens, the expression itself. It is illustrated as follows.

---

6. See: *Neptune in Focus,* forthcoming by the author.

The family is playing tennis in the park (a shared moment).

The grandmother is at home baking bread, or maybe drinking tea or water, or maybe she has gone shopping.

There is uncertainty.

The family does not really know, because it is the grandmother's moment.

The moment of the tennis game is relative to events in other peoples' lives.

The tennis game passes and remains as a family memory.

It remains in the sixth dimension.

The moment for the grandmother is also in the sixth dimension.

Unless the sixth dimension is accessed, which is similar to turning on a television monitor and witnessing an event, expressions of energy, or individual moments, remain unknown to others because natal patterns respond differently to prevailing cosmic energy influences. In human terms everyone experiences each moment differently.

The linking nature of cosmic energy extends moments beyond a single dimension. Links to other dimensions permit connection, but not necessarily access. Dimension access occurs in a similar way that a computer functions: although a computer is linked to a particular data base, access is only through a special code. Energy directions which extend into other dimensions link the present with the past or the future. Humans experience stirrings of ancient memories or déjà vu.

Memory is associated with the sixth dimension.

Recall, or prediction, depends on access; it is not always accurate.

CONCEPT: The sixth dimension is a memory.

Momentary Cosmic Energy Structure

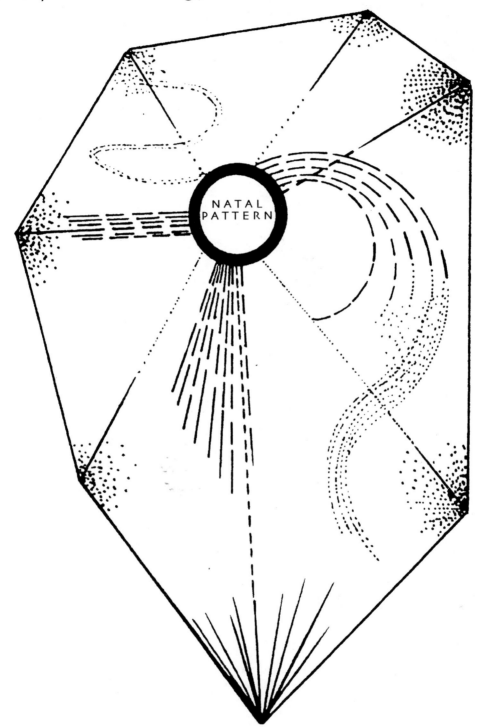

NATAL
PATTERN

Momentary Energy Shape

The shape of the moment contains all the interacting energies.

Crystalline Corridor

Cosmic energy passes through dimensions many times.

A momentary energy shape is similar to a crystal because cosmic energy arrives on Earth in angular directions. This means that momentary sequence causes dimensions to form like a crystalline corridor—a spiraling tunnel through which cosmic energy continually passes.

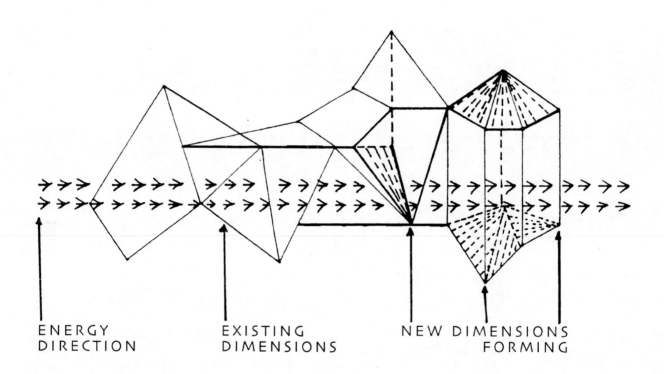

ENERGY
DIRECTION

EXISTING
DIMENSIONS

NEW DIMENSIONS
FORMING

Dimensions Are Like Crystals

The dimensions of a natal pattern life-cycle are like a crystalline corridor. Each dimension has a particular shape formed by energy interaction in the moment, and is, therefore, identified by a specific energy imprint. As cosmic bodies cycle, cosmic energy passes through these shapes. New dimensions are created as different energy links form.

Dimension Recognition

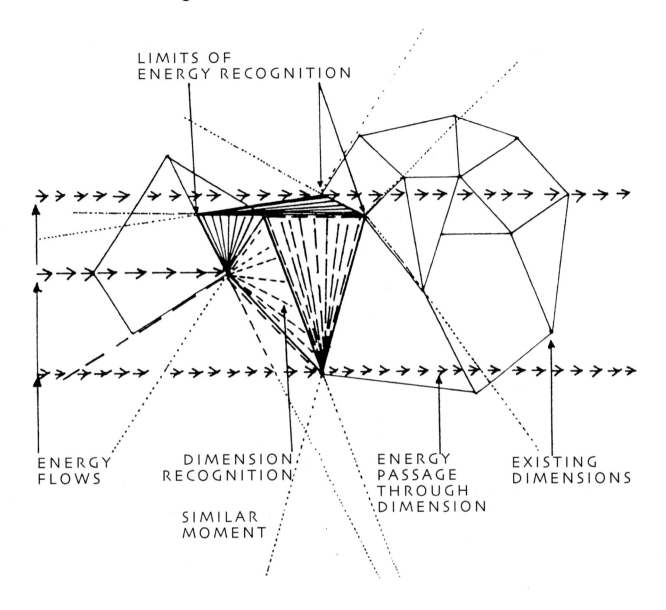

LIMITS OF
ENERGY RECOGNITION

ENERGY
FLOWS

DIMENSION
RECOGNITION

SIMILAR
MOMENT

ENERGY
PASSAGE
THROUGH
DIMENSION

EXISTING
DIMENSIONS

Cosmic Energy Recognizes Shape

The above illustration shows the passage of energy through a dimension. Similar energy identifies a shape. As cosmic energy connects with sensitive points, dimension recognition occurs in a similar moment. Energy recognition allows humans to experience familiarity. Familiarity allows memory access. Every year the Earth passes through the shapes, or dimensions, of our birthdays. Cosmic energy continues to pass through other dimensions, as though nothing were happening. Without connection cosmic energy continues to pass through dimensions as though they were non-existent.

Past/Present/Future

Past, present, and future are dimensions from different perspectives.

As cosmic energy passes from moment to moment in the continuous process of energy alignments, cosmic links connect past, present, and future in the different dimensions of time.

In cosmic terms the past is the space from which energy has moved; the present is the space in which energy is moving; the future is the space into which energy will move. As energy approaches the future, the past recedes from energy expression in the present.

Each dimension corresponds to a moment of energy expression. As energy continues to move in space and express itself in new moments, it merely distances itself from any particular moment in a past dimension. Eventually, on any cycle, the past is at the maximum distance from the present at which point it becomes a future dimension to which energy is beginning an approach. Since all energy cycles, eventually past dimensions (now in the future), will be occupied by energy in the present.[7] If a momentary energy structure fits the shape of a previous dimension, the energy expression will repeat itself. More frequently, shapes are not exactly the same. However, at particular cyclical intervals energy patterns reoccur and momentary shapes are similar. Similar events happen again. History seems to be replayed. Within a human lifetime overlay phenomena will modify memory, but similarity should not go unnoticed.[8] As energy expresses itself, each moment becomes part of the universal memory—the collective consciousness which exists forever.

CONCEPT: The past pervades the present.

In physical reality the present is always now.

While I write, a child is sleeping, people are drinking beer, traffic is crossing a bridge.

I am in my present moment of existence: I am in now. Others are in other dimensions inaccessible to me, but very real and the present for them. Later, if others tell me what happened, it is recalled; it is from the past. If they tell me what they plan, it is in the future. Only the telling is now; the rest is in other dimensions.

CONCEPT: Now is a dimension, an energy shape in space, a position of energy expression in physical reality, the moment itself.

---

7. See "Merge Point" on page 143.
8. See Concept on page 84, and "Similarity" on page 81.

Perspective

The Dimensions of Time are like Multiple Window Frames

Imagine standing in a window frame and surveying the scene from that position.

The illustration shows in symbolic form a person standing in a window frame, then moving into the adjacent frame which is in a slightly different position. The view is different and the perspective of the first frame changes, as does the third window frame into which the person next moves. Little by little, as the person enters different window frames, the perspective changes. The dimensions of time are similar. It is how a person moves through space.

The person is in the present in frame 1. It is equivalent to the moment of energy expression now. Being in frame 13 represents the future. When the person arrives in frame 13, frames 1 to 12 are in the past. The person has passed through space, creating time in the process. The passage is in other dimensions in universal terms and in the dimension of memory for the person. The passage continues to exist in the sixth dimension.

Perspective may be described as a point of view, literally, a view from a point.

The motion of the Earth may be interpreted in terms of the Earth continually moving away from where it was. As it moves into space, the Earth is also approaching where it will be. All other cosmic bodies are also moving. Past, present, and future exist because cosmic energy is moving.

When it is no longer now, time has not passed; it is merely no longer the present dimension for a particular energy expression. The event has happened. It is already in the past. Yet it once existed and, therefore, once was. It exists now in another dimension. Everything exists now and in another dimension at the same time, depending on perspective. Considered from other dimensions, events have not occurred, occurred in distant antiquity, occurred recently, or are imminent. Only for those involved in an event is it now. To someone who is in the present, what has happened is in the past. What is yet to happen is in the future. To someone who is still in the future, something in the present is in the past. To someone who is in the past, something in the present is in the future. The perspective from the future shows the past as the future because energy cycles.

The path of impending energy expression shows the past as energy expressed, the present as energy expressing, and the future as energy yet to be expressed.

That the past "has gone" does not imply finality. Moments in the past were essential for moments to unfold in the present and future. In the movement of energy into space, the future becomes the past and will eventually become the present again in the continuing cycles of energy expression. The natal pattern predominates; only details are different in the cosmic energy continuum.[9]

Common Dimension

The past and the future merge at a point equidistant from now.

In a lineal context, the past has gone and the future has not happened; the two can never meet. In a circular context, the past and future are positions on a cycle. At a common point, equidistant from the present, they become a single dimension. Whatever the cyclical interval, the position of the present was once the position of a common dimension, a merge point where cosmic energy links the present with both the past and the future. In this way, the present moment is linked to more than one dimension, since all positions on any cycle have been past and future merge points and will be again.

Thus, the past and future continually merge in the present. This phenomenon allows an individual to connect with past lives through energy links with different dimensions. "Old souls" meet again. It means an individual can recapture knowledge and skills from previous lifetimes, which are observed in natural ability and in exceptionally gifted children. Different cycles and, therefore, energy combinations, provide the opportunity to gain wisdom through many experiences.

CONCEPT: Every position on every energy cycle represents a past/future merge point

---

9. See "Energy Moves into Space" on page 107; and "Common Dimension" on page 141.

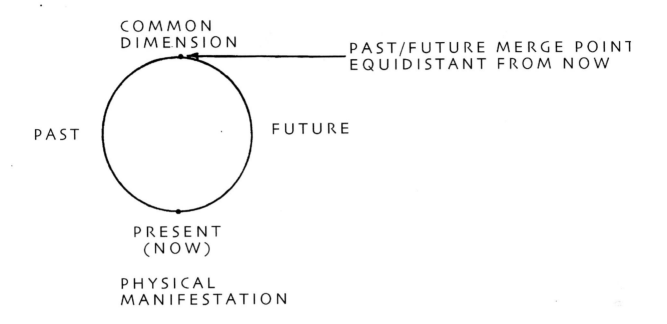

Common Dimension

The future is always adjacent to the past at the focus point equidistant from the present (now). A position exists on every energy cycle where the past and future are one. Therefore, all positions contain past and future dimensions.

CONCEPT: The past pervades the present.

The Past Pervades the Present

In this illustration, the past contains a forest; the present contains a building in a clearing. The site is the same. The building now dominates this scene. The past is in non-physical reality; the present is in physical reality now. Both exist in different dimensions of time.

Merge Point

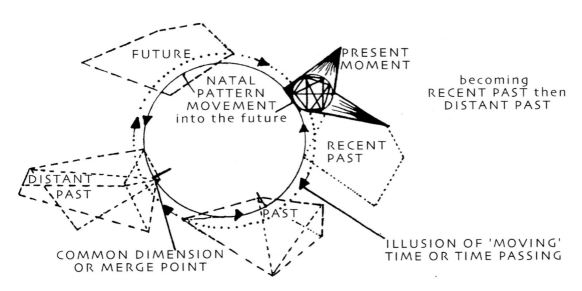

This illustration shows the different dimensions of time, where the distant past and distant future occupy a common position and are, therefore, one at the merge point

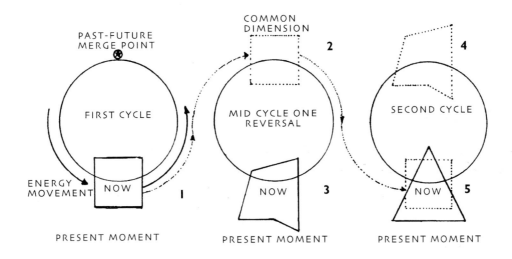

The above illustration shows movement of energy. On any cycle the present moment (1) is as far in energy distance from the past as the future. The opposing position to the present (2) is the past/future merge point—a common dimension which contains a specific energy imprint.

At mid-cycle these two positions are reversed. What was "now" (1) is the common dimension (2) at the past/future merge position. The past/future dimension pervades the present (3) the moment itself. At full cycle, the common dimension (2) has returned to pervade the present moment again (5). There is a similar energy expression, another imprint. Energy continues to move in a second cycle ad infinitum.

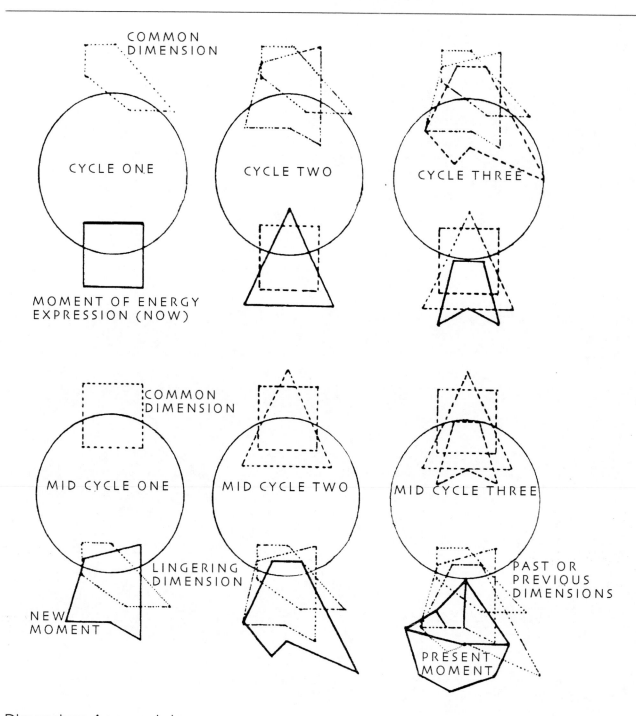

Dimensions Accumulate

This illustration shows the accumulation of dimensions due to their lingering nature and how the past pervades the present. In the diagram each moment of energy expression (now) is drawn as a simple geometric shape. This shape remains as a dimension. At mid-cycle, this momentary shape represents a common dimension at the past/future merge point.

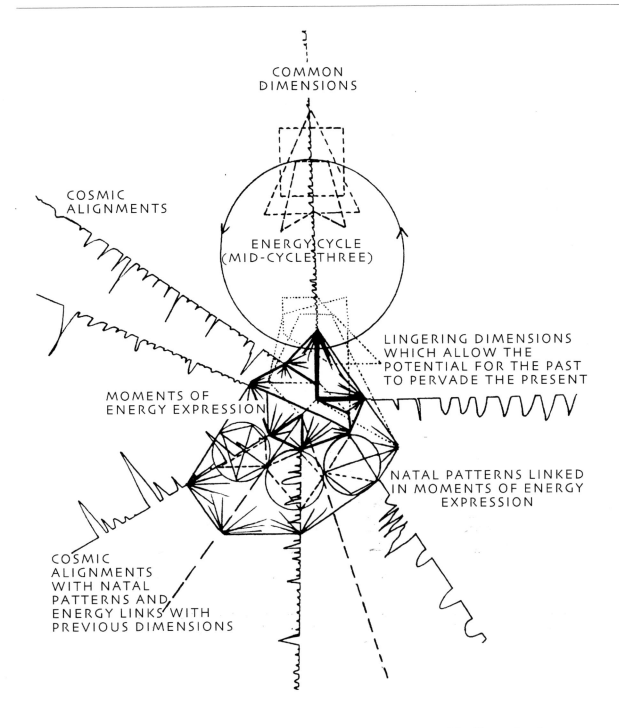

COMMON
DIMENSIONS

COSMIC
ALIGNMENTS

ENERGY CYCLE
(MID-CYCLE THREE)

LINGERING DIMENSIONS
WHICH ALLOW THE
POTENTIAL FOR THE PAST
TO PERVADE THE PRESENT

MOMENTS OF
ENERGY EXPRESSION

NATAL PATTERNS LINKED
IN MOMENTS OF ENERGY
EXPRESSION

COSMIC
ALIGNMENTS
WITH NATAL
PATTERNS AND
ENERGY LINKS WITH
PREVIOUS DIMENSIONS

This diagram expands the detail of MID CYCLE THREE from the previous page. The illustration shows two moments of energy expression in which three natal patterns interact with each other. Each pattern is linked to the cosmos and previous dimensions during the connection process. Energy links occur through sensitive points according to cosmic configuration and natal pattern codes.

All Dimensions Co-Exist

This illustration shows the complexity of dimension accumulation and the potential for multi-dimensional linking. The circle represents the path of a natal pattern in the daily cycle (once round the Earth).

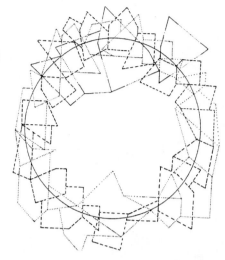

Multi-Dimensional Linking

Dimensions accumulate.

Dimensions are invisible energy codes which accumulate as natal patterns interact with the cosmos. They may be considered like time tanks. Most people (natal patterns) are unaware that these dimensions exist, just as most of us are unaware of our natal patterns.

The existence of dimensions provides the framework for multi-dimensional linking, the phenomenon which allows memory, ideas, inventions, and pre-cognition. The process is mostly instantaneous, which explains the "flash of insight," the sudden leap in the mind, and, in particular, access to channeled information. Without cosmic links natal patterns move freely through dimensions as though they did not exist.

A moment exists forever in another dimension.

Moments of energy expression depend upon linking within energy arrangements. How cosmic energy manifests depends on the energy principles and the cycles which also bring dimensions into the arena of connection.

In the moment of energy expression, particular energy can link many dimensions together which allows the past, present, or future to pervade the present moment. A common principle which occurs at energy return facilitates this linking. As the cosmos rearranges itself, energy links are released. Particular dimensions separate from the moment. Dimension access may be difficult because so many dimensions co-exist and are superimposed upon each other.

Different dimensions allow physical existence within non-physical reality and non-physical existence in reality.

Dimension Specificity

Similarity

"...and there is nothing new under the sun."

Ecclesiastes 1:8

Dimensions retain energy sensitivity after cosmic energy has moved on. In this way dimensions are memories—residual energy sensitive spaces, shapes through which cosmic energy continues to pass, again and again, just as the Earth passes through the dimensions of our birthday every year.

During energy return, an energy principle is emphasized. At the individual level, the natal pattern experiences similarity. A similar response to cosmic energy causes expression in a very similar way reminiscent of earlier life, such as childhood—similar characters reappear; similar events happen.[10] Vast cycles are involved which link the present with the past. In human terms, people visit historic places, Stonehenge, Machu Picchu, the Greek Islands, mostly unaware of the cyclical connection or particular energy return. This means that over millennia, things on Earth reoccur in a similar way, until a major cosmic upheaval changes the entire energy structure.

Energy recognition of a dimension imprint allows humans to experience familiarity.

CONCEPT: Cosmic energy passes through dimensions which have existed since antiquity.

Psychic Phenomena

Inevitability

Inevitability allows precognition.

Cosmic patterns which have already existed and interacted, and those which will exist and interact, are inevitable arrangements of cosmic bodies due to their motion. As the Earth forms angular relationships to other cosmic bodies, inevitable arrangements must, and will, occur. In turn, the different combinations of cosmic emissions exert influences; their effect causes events on Earth. The process is a continuum of cosmic body cycles, cosmic energy patterns, and cosmic energy interaction.

Cyclical energy movement permits the past and future to meet and merge continually in each moment of energy expression where each moment defines a dimension. In this context, there is no difference between prophecy and memory recall, for both are dimension imprints—energy sensitive shapes, or energy codes, attached to cycles.

Cosmic energy is either approaching or receding from a position on a cycle. All moments and, therefore, events, occupy a position in a sequence. In this way cosmic energy

---

10. See "Similarity" on page 81; and Stock Market Crashes #1: Black Monday, 1929 and #2: Black Friday October 13, 1989.

allows the phenomenon of precognition or past-life regression. Prediction, precognition, and/or prophecy is the reverse direction of memory recall.

PRINCIPLE: Cosmic configuration is inevitable.
CONCEPT: Inevitability allows precognition.

Precognition

Cosmic patterns allow psychic access.

Knowing something before it happens (pre-cognition) is often surrounded by doubt, mystery, and awe, due largely to a lack of comprehension. Knowing something after it happens is accepted readily because it was witnessed and is remembered. Precognition is through dimension access. The process is possible because cosmic configuration is inevitable. Psychic perception is the ability to connect with another dimension. The phenomenon of prediction, or past-life regression, is a cosmic energy process which hinges on dimension imprint or shape, which identifies an energy code.[11]

Everything has an energy shape.[12] Even though we cannot see it, the shape still exists. Shapes occur through cosmic energy arrangement. Without energy, shape does not exist. Each dimension represents a structural shape. In this way a dimension may be accessed by energy. Dimension access allows a past moment to be viewed again as in video films, a present moment to be witnessed by millions as in television, and a future moment to be predicted by psychics or mediums.[13]

Certain individuals, with perception beyond the usual range (the fifth dimension), show in their abilities that existence is far more than the physical world, and that it is possible to access a point in time or a shape in space which has not yet arrived or has passed. For the psychic to know the future or the past, the events must have an energy code that can be accessed. Certain energy arrangements allow connections which access dimension imprints, or impending momentary shapes. Psychics connect with other dimensions through focus, which detects a shape and position similar to a radar scanner and sense events concerning an individual's life in both the future and the past. Psychics use this process, but may not know how it works. Psychics access dimensions through cosmic energy linking.

CONCEPT: Precognition is through dimension access.

11. See "6D" on page 124.
12. See "Crystalline Concept" on page 20.
13. See "CONCEPT: Inevitability." on page 184.

Psychic Connection

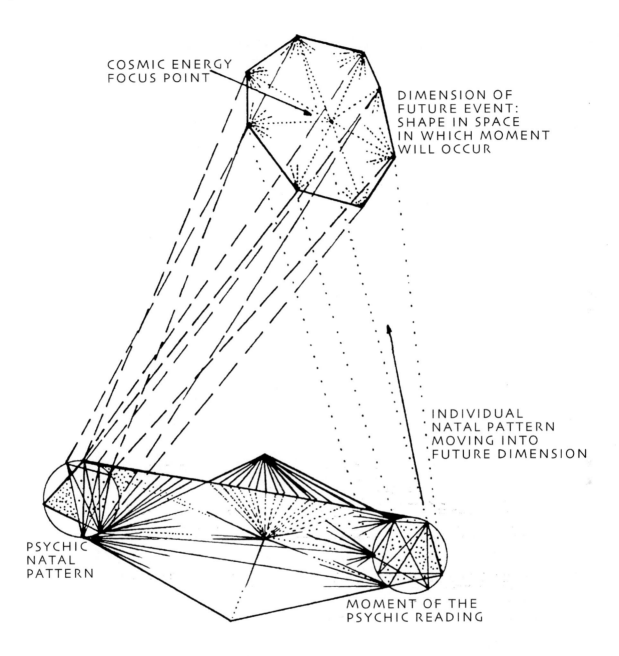

COSMIC ENERGY
FOCUS POINT

DIMENSION OF
FUTURE EVENT:
SHAPE IN SPACE
IN WHICH MOMENT
WILL OCCUR

INDIVIDUAL
NATAL PATTERN
MOVING INTO
FUTURE DIMENSION

PSYCHIC
NATAL
PATTERN

MOMENT OF THE
PSYCHIC READING

Psychics Access Dimensions Through Cosmic Energy Linking

This symbolic illustration shows a psychic connection with a shape or future dimension into which an individual will move. The psychic and individual connect in the moment of the reading through particular sensitive points in each pattern.

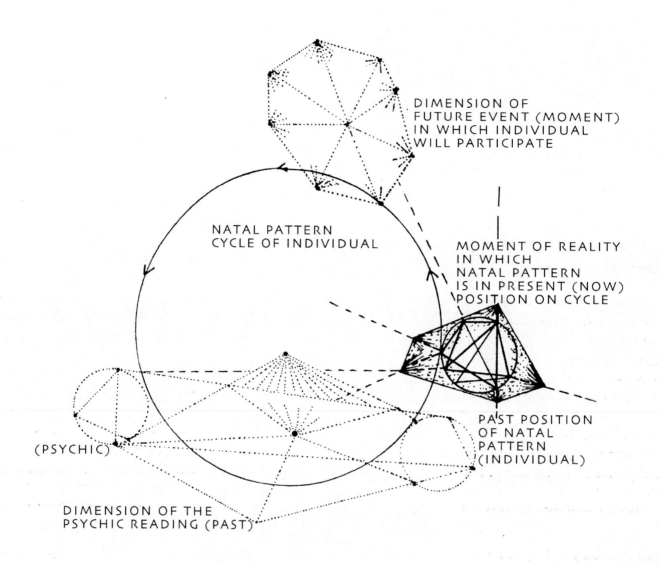

DIMENSION OF
FUTURE EVENT (MOMENT)
IN WHICH INDIVIDUAL
WILL PARTICIPATE

NATAL PATTERN
CYCLE OF INDIVIDUAL

MOMENT OF REALITY
IN WHICH
NATAL PATTERN
IS IN PRESENT (NOW)
POSITION ON CYCLE

(PSYCHIC)

PAST POSITION
OF NATAL
PATTERN
(INDIVIDUAL)

DIMENSION OF THE
PSYCHIC READING (PAST)

The Moment of the Psychic Reading Has Passed

The illustration shows that past, present, and future moments are each in a different dimension and in different positions on the cycle of the individual.

Dimension Overload

"One Christmas was so much like another."

Dylan Thomas
A Child's Christmas in Wales

Moments erase memories through superimposition.

For each natal pattern, each time a moment occurs the energy structure superimposes itself on existing dimensions in that position. In this process of space definition by moments of energy expression, dimensions can fill space with energy imprints like data banks become overloaded with codes of information. Dimension overload masks detailed definition—things become blurred. It means that gradually energy expression masks everything because dimension overload impedes accessibility.[14] That time blots out memories or heals all things refers to this phenomenon. It is particularly evident when very similar moments are repeated frequently. The most common example happens during the daily cycle; the day-to-day life which for particular, or prolonged, periods is very similar. Long, stable periods in life often result in the inability to remember clearly, or distinguish one day from another. Only exceptional events are remembered with accuracy.[15] Rare events remain clear due to uniqueness, or an uncluttered time such as occurs in childhood. Unless what happens is significant enough to the individual, such as a birthday of special meaning, the past memory merges into generality. The present associates past events (previous birthdays) and there is not a fresh imprint for special recall. A psychic collects information from a space shape. When that point is overloaded, exact timing and details are difficult to discern because space definition is blurred. Dimension overload explains why older folk have difficulty distinguishing each separate birthday. The young child easily recovers the memory and recalls the details.

If dimension access by energy were perfected by humans, recall would be exact for everything which ever occurred.

14. See "Dissimilarity obscures energy return." on page 86.
15. See "Ski-Lift Analogy" on page 108; and "Masking" on page 152.

Masking

Masking may occur during cycle overlay.

Points of energy return are positions of specific energy superimposition. Frequent cycles reach these points often and are easily recognized, such as an anniversary. The more frequent the cycle, the more superimposition occurs because the position is passed so many times. The similarity of so many energy imprints makes it difficult to distinguish one dimension from another.

Psychics have difficulty pin-pointing time when (the 5th dimension) due to dimension overlay. Moments at the same time of year (the same solar position on the Earth's cycle) may cause blurring to the psychic. Distinguishing an order of events is difficult because of the identical position in space and similarity of shape. For this reason when each of several events are to occur for an individual, all in summertime, the psychic often finds it difficult to distinguish which event will occur in which year. The psychic can detect the time of year (common connecting principle, the sun) but not, necessarily, which year; three consecutive summers may merge in the forecast. When three events will occur "next summer" it may also mean that in the next three consecutive summers one of each event will occur; thus, the interval is extended and what is to happen takes longer.

Psychic error in timing is due to cycle overlay.

Access

Universal memory is stored in dimensions.

A dimension is an invisible shape which remains within the system as an energy-sensitive space, a cosmic code that depends on energy focus points and sensitive positions in space. Each dimension is unique and may be accessed by energy in particular ways, which means that events may be recovered through a medium, television, photography, or human memory. All dimensions hinge on one another, but linking is only through energy. At particular cyclical intervals, dimensions may be activated like the reiteration of a speech, the recital of a poem, or the re-enactment of a play. Through dimension access by means of cosmic energy, knowledge, skills, and wisdom may be retrieved from dimensions which have existed since antiquity. Projection into future dimensions allows inventions, new theories, and new techniques.

CONCEPT: Cognition is a cosmic energy process.

Timing

The cosmos is an energy system.
Psychics and astrologers are part of this system.
Both use specific skills to identify events.
Both will eventually arrive at the same conclusion
For a moment occurs at an energy focus point in space.

The psychic is like a dancer
without a sense of timing who knows the steps are coming.
The astrologer is like a drummer
who is always on time because he knows about energy cycles.

The natal pattern waits to dance the steps to come,
with energy for each movement and in perfect choreographic detail
within the rhythm of the cosmos.

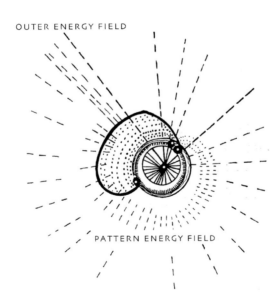

The Natal Pattern is Multidimensional and Allows Access From Other Dimensions And Into Other Realms

This symbolic illustration shows a resonating natal pattern pulsing in space time. It involves shape, configuration, centers, and antennae receptors which can penetrate other dimensions.

Analogies: 1) Jellyfish in clear sea water. Simple energy pattern in vast ocean. 2) Planet Earth in cosmos. Highly complex energy pattern in intricate, elaborate energy field.

Twelve • Synchronicity

Synchronicity is the principle of timing.

Synchronicity, or cosmic timing, is an integral part of cosmic rhythm and the prerequisite for everything which happens on Earth. It is the reason why everything occurs exactly when it does. Based on alignments between revolving energy sources and sensitive point positions in natal patterns on Earth, synchronicity is the essential factor in cosmic connection which allows natal patterns to meet and interact.

Although a cosmic encounter brings patterns together, interaction in the moment is determined by energy principles. Combinations of energy principles are dependent on the synchronized movement of energy cycles, where each moment is a focus point for converging cosmic energy. In this way, energy cycles control each moment on Earth through timing: whom we meet, when and where and for how long our lives are entwined. Just as the cosmos can bring someone and something into our lives, it can also remove them. When connection is denied, particular patterns cannot interact. What might have happened does not unfold: a potential moment does not occur. For this reason a moment involves the deeper meaning of existence, or destiny, which is linked to karma through the planet Saturn, Kronos the timer. [1]

Thus, synchronicity is fundamental to energy expression in each moment.

Coincidence

Coincidence is an energy phenomenon.

Coincidence is a feature of synchronicity and, therefore, energy cycle dependent.[2] It occurs when cycles converge. In this way energy cycles control timing.

CONCEPT: Moments occur at coinciding energy focus points (to be differentiated from coinciding moments which occur at the same time).

---

1. See "Saturn delays." on page 61; and "Destiny is linked to karma through Saturn in the natal pattern." on page 187.
2. See "Cosmic Rhythm" on page 75.

Luggage Analogy

Energy cycles are like circular conveyor belts carrying luggage at the airport. Sometimes all the luggage arrives at once. Sometimes there is a delay when the conveyor belt stops but, eventually, the luggage moves again. Sometimes the suitcases arrive slowly. One can see them approaching long before it is possible to accept them. Sometimes a suitcase passes by, out of reach, or in the moment one bends to tie a shoelace. Eventually the suitcases and person coincide.

Things come to us in life in the same way. Although we may spend time searching, trying to control events, and attempting to bring to ourselves what we think is needed in the moment, everything arrives in cosmic time, when we are ready.

The Universal Excuse

Old philosophies state that the teacher appears when the student is ready. This is the point of readiness, the time for it to happen. Readiness is frequently observed in the timing of events on Earth. In times of war or crisis, the leaders appear miraculously, as if from nowhere, just as the need arises. Does the need create the leader? Or does the leader create the need? Neither is correct, for the leader is already preparing and reaching the point of readiness. The crisis is imminent; synchronicity brings the two together.

Humans often notice that timing coincides with mutual need within the system. It is observed that when shelter is needed, a room becomes available; when jobs are required work appears. In a similar way, without something to build construction workers cannot pursue their trades; without a construction crew, a house will not be built.

Coincidence is like a universal excuse which may hide or mask the purpose of interaction which involves the deeper meaning of existence.

Duality

Duality pervades all things like an unwritten law

The universe is dual in its nature. It is a system of energy processes that range between opposites: connection and disconnection, fusion and division. This duality is reflected in all of its parts.

Polarity

Polarity is a feature of cosmic duality.

"Poles Apart" is an idiomatic description of the underlying universal principle of polarity, which allows energy to express itself between two extremes: activity, inactivity; joy, sorrow; belief, doubt. Cosmic energy, like electrical and magnetic energy, exhibits polarity as it constantly oscillates between opposites. Its movement reflects the dual nature of the universe in a system of energy confinement and release. Energy occupies space and withdraws; expands and contracts; culminates and declines in a perpetual rhythm of cosmic cycles. The effect on Earth is easily recognized in the ebb and flow of ocean tides, the movement of human lungs, the waxing and waning of the moon. Moments on Earth reflect this tug of polarity: the expression of masculinity and femininity, of kindness and cruelty, of wealth and poverty.

Life on Earth lives in a narrow band—a sphere of relatively gentle energy interaction like a middle pH value, sometimes slightly acidic, sometimes a little alkaline.

Extreme energy expression is seen in the forces which create land upheavals: volcanic eruptions, mountain ranges, rift valley subsidence. For a while, like storms in local areas, there is a raging fury. In the calm of the aftermath, life as we know it exists and evolves.

SYMBOLIC CONCEPT OF DUALITY

But the energy which allows it to be….
    which is essential,
    that is the essence of all things continues…
    bringing massing and dissipating,
    gathering and scattering,
    interaction and inactivity.
    The constant tug is energy:
    active and finding expression.
    Polarity must always be balanced.

Significance

Time is a mosaic of moments in which all are significant. The moments are like pieces in a vast multidimensional jigsaw puzzle in motion—there is a position for each piece which must be acknowledged. Without each piece, the puzzle is incomplete. Everything is linked and needed and part of the total: talking to a waitress at a cafe table, standing next to shoppers at a cash register, sitting beside a stranger on a ski-lift, seeing people one may never see again. What does it mean? These chance encounters may seem unimportant, yet they are essential moments. However insignificant a moment may seem it serves as a necessary link in the synchronicity and complexity of the whole.

When an old woman is passing in front of a car, the car and its occupants must wait and allow her to pass; there is time for her. This seemingly insignificant incident may appear to be inconsequential: an occurrence which might pass unnoticed, or is briefly observed and then dismissed. The moment may serve to remind one of those older, wiser, perhaps less fortunate, or more privileged, than oneself. Even the thought in that instant may be of value to the thinker. The incident may serve as a delay in a schedule so that one avoids something else. Should the delay have prevented a car accident, the incident would gain in significance. One would recount the tale and feel fortunate. One would remember the old woman who passed in front of a car.[3] At another time, the old woman will wait for a car to pass.

Energy expression depends on connection. Each moment of energy expression is part of universal timing and makes a contribution. For everyone, each moment precedes the next. Each causes one to be delayed just enough, so that one will be at another place exactly when one should. Perhaps someone who needed a little more time to arrive will be there. What seems to be a delay for some, allows for those about to be encountered, to proceed in their own moment: on schedule for them and for the seemingly delayed to remain within the moment of individual existence.

As our galaxy hurtles into the vastness of space, we should remember we are part of this motion. We occupy a position in space and exist for a few moments in which we interact with others. Encounters may be brief, but each one is significant. Each individual is as necessary as another, regardless of different life directions.

Everything in the universe is in motion. All movement is relative to everything else.

Inclusion

Moments are part of the lives of others, as well as oneself, and illustrate the principle of inclusion. The significance is that we are all part of one system. Everything belongs—we must all fit into the cosmic mosaic. In the rush of everyday life, it is easy to miss a seemingly insignificant moment. A simple statement, a casual remark, even a single word is enough to initiate a flow of thoughts which can have far-reaching consequences. The flash of insight on

---

3. At the intersection lights in Pitt River, British Columbia, the author waited as an old woman crossed the road very slowly. Her face inspired this page.

the prepared mind, like a depressed key which sets into motion a chain of connections, could happen at anytime. Since every moment is a potential for this, every moment matters because each is a nucleus for further energy expression. With the knowledge that as one moment leads into the next, each moment makes a contribution, the whole concept of time changes. There is no frantic rush; all will occur as it should in its own moment.

Within the dimensions of time, there is enough time for everything: each thought, each word, each deed. There is a time for each moment. Everything happens as it should and when it should, in sequence. Everything is timed to the fraction of a second. An event occurs in its own time, at the precise moment. The individual cannot accelerate or delay it.[4]

"To every thing there is a season, and a time to every purpose under the heaven:

A time to be born, and a time to die;
a time to plant, and a time to pluck up that which is planted;

A time to kill, and a time to heal;
a time to break down, and a time to build up;

A time to weep, and a time to laugh;
a time to mourn, and a time to dance;

A time to cast away stones, and a time to gather stones together;
a time to embrace, and a time to refrain from embracing;

A time to get, and a time to lose;
a time to keep, and a time to cast away;

A time to rend, and a time to sew;
a time to keep silence, and a time to speak;

A time to love, and a time to hate;
a time of war, and a time of peace."

Ecclesiastes 3: 1-8

---

4. See "Suggested Reading," Barbara Hand Clow, p. 203.

Summary for Part Two

Time does not pass.
Energy moves in space.
Time is fixed in the moment of energy expression.
A moment is a shape in space: an interval in the fourth dimension, a synchronized rhythm in the fifth dimension, a memory in the sixth dimension.[5]

---

5. These concepts change our familiar comprehension of time.

Thirteen • Man in the System

Concept

"We are nothing more than unified energy fields."

Barbara Hand Clow
Chiron[1]

Uniqueness

Humans are biological forms of cosmic energy.

In human terms, an individual is a person. In cosmic terms, an individual is an energy pattern, a code which represents a cosmic configuration that momentarily existed in the heavens. As such, an individual reflects a cosmic moment and is unique.

In physical form, humans do not reveal their energy codes. However, physical traits and behavior offer clues, because all human shapes exhibit features characteristic of planetary energies and zodiacal position.[2] Even though we all change during our lifetime, particularly physically, the one thing that remains constant is our natal pattern. In repeated cycles over millions of years, the influence of prevailing cosmic forces in millions of moments, has contributed to the huge range of human diversity, just as the arrangement of energy in the natal pattern determines the individuality, or uniqueness, of each human being in a single moment on Earth.

The glamorous film star, the deep-sea diver, the lonely shepherd are natal patterns captured in human form, or cosmic energy personified.

What needs to be realized is that an individual, neither more nor less than anything else, is an energy pattern and that, when cosmic energy rearranges itself in a particular way, the physical body disintegrates because the natal pattern can no longer sustain itself in that particular form. The outward manifestation, or life experience, is death.

Although the moment of energy expression is a geometrical shape because exact alignments form angular shapes, orbital motion causes curves in physical reality. As moments occur and momentary shapes change, the effect of the moment lingers in the familiar shapes on Earth.

---

1. See "Suggested Reading," Barbara Hand Clow, p. 203.
2. See "Suggested Reading," Astrological Keywords, p. 203.

CONCEPTS: Biophysical individuality is due to cosmic uniqueness.

Astrophysical uniqueness is dependent on cosmic energy arrangement.

Cosmic energy affects everything.

Everything on Earth represents a pattern of energy. Nothing is excluded. At all times cosmic energy is exerting an influence on these patterns. For this reason, human beings and cosmic influences cannot be separated. The two are entwined in a permanent relationship which dictates how everything will unfold. Humans are continually confronted by a bombardment of cosmic emissions, yet are generally unaware of the presence of cosmic energy. Nevertheless, this energy affects the way we feel, respond, and behave.

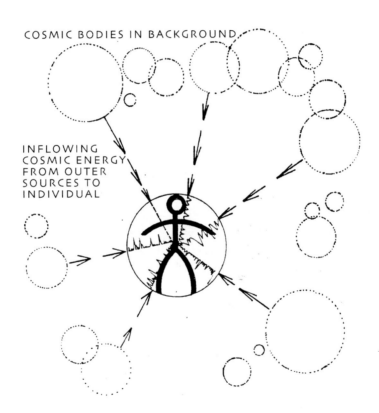

COSMIC BODIES IN BACKGROUND

INFLOWING COSMIC ENERGY FROM OUTER SOURCES TO INDIVIDUAL

Each Human Being is a Focus Point or Receptor for Cosmic Energy. Each Vibrates According to a Frequency Unique to the Pattern.

The individual is in a constantly changing energy field.[3]

---

3. See "All Things Exist In A Cosmic Energy Shape" on page 4.

Crystal Analogy

Natal patterns are like crystals in motion.

A human natal pattern may be likened to a moving crystal which turns different facets to different things. Each facet "looks at" what it faces and "sees" different things simultaneously. Similarly, each individual reflects personality in a complex imagery, as a crystal refracts and reflects light.

Most of us may be compared to simple crystals, like sodium chloride, which has only a few facets. Complex people are like complex crystals which have many facets. Each "crystal face" interacts, or offers a multi-reflective system, indicative of a complex, or intricate structure. The more complex an individual, the more "faces" there are to expose to the outside world.

At all times, each individual reflects and reveals different "faces" and in this shows different personality traits. Most individuals only ever see one or a few faces of everyone else; the other "faces" are never revealed because they "look" another way. The "face," or side, of an individual which is shown, and, therefore, shared, is directly linked to the natal pattern which determines connections with others.

Peak performance of an individual is like the full brilliance of total reflection. The crystal sparkles and shines; cosmic energy is in its optimum state. Many individuals operate only in part, as though much of their system is closed, like a raw crystal which needs faceting.

A natal pattern, like a crystal, will only be of its type, a pre-determined structure. Common salt will never become a diamond.

Human Focus Points

Natal patterns are cosmic energy focus points.

Each human being is a focus point for cosmic energy, a natal pattern which vibrates according to a frequency unique to the pattern. Each frequency obeys astrological energy principles and connects with the cosmos in a particular way. Cosmic energy links all patterns to the cosmic grid, providing connection channels among focus points. As a cosmic energy focus point, each natal pattern functions as an energy transformer and may be compared to a substation in an electrical grid in which all units are needed for maximum power. Malfunction of a unit affects the whole. Numerous malfunctioning units upset equilibrium forcing correction. Similarly, each human being contributes to the cosmic energy grid.

Everything which happens makes a contribution to the cosmic energy system and is a portion of something much greater than itself. Man is part of this system. In this acceptance, each individual is part of the cosmos in a positive, or willing, sense. Each has a place, a position, a space to fill and a role to play. The process is analogous to a play in which each player is assigned to a role that is to be played out to the finale. The best play is well rehearsed and well executed, with each player giving his best performance. To play one's part fully is to accept and know it thoroughly. Non-acceptance causes frustration, irritation, and anger and is a negative manifestation of cosmic energy and, therefore, works against the self, because it is working essentially against the system in which, inevitably, cosmic law will prevail.[4]

Man exists in an energy system, but has not yet learned to live with its power.

4. See "Nothing happens by chance." on page 44.

Fourteen • Lifecycle

Concept

A Lifepath is an Energy Spiral

A lifetime represents many rotations with the Earth.

A lifetime is the movement of a natal pattern in space. The path is an energy direction formed by a sequence of moments which spiral around the sun. Each moment leaves a dimension, a residual shape defined by an energy imprint. Thus, the shape of a lifetime is the defined space in which a natal pattern interacts with cosmic energy as it rotates with the Earth.

If the Earth were stationary in orbit, one rotation on its axis would bring any Earth point to its starting position in space. However, the Earth is also moving around the sun, so that each Earth point misses exact connection with its starting position. In this way, the path of a natal pattern is a spiral in space because each natal pattern identifies with a point on Earth. If a natal pattern remains in the same location on Earth, it retraces or superimposes its path each year. Since all cosmic bodies are gradually changing their positions relative to each other, the energy influences on Earth are also changing as energy principles are rearranged. Thus, each year the natal pattern is influenced differently. Through multiple rotations, each natal pattern enriches its cosmic energy experience. The human experience is "growing up" and "growing old," which reflects the cyclical principle of culmination and decline.

A lifepath refers to an energy direction known as destiny. Metaphorically, it is often called a journey.

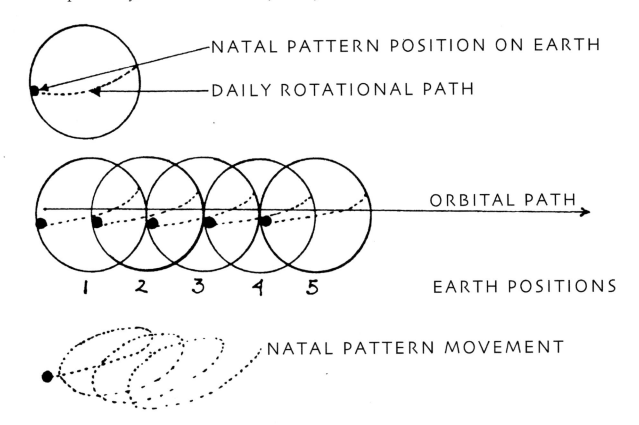

NATAL PATTERN POSITION ON EARTH

DAILY ROTATIONAL PATH

ORBITAL PATH

EARTH POSITIONS

NATAL PATTERN MOVEMENT

A natal pattern spins with the Earth and gradually moves around the sun. The path is a spiral in space.

Allotted Time

A lifetime is a dimension in the cosmos.

Moments within a lifetime, and the lifetime itself, are all energy arrangements in space because moments are created by energy expression.

A lifetime represents a shape in the cosmos, an allotted time fixed for each of us by our natal pattern. As we move through life, we create the dimension of our own reality. Some natal patterns pass quickly through the moments of a lifetime, other patterns are retained for longer. Eventually, all energy moves away.

A lifetime is a dimension in the shape of a crystalline corridor through which cosmic energy passes. In human experience, it seems lineal due to sequential energy expression. However, a lifetime is cyclical, involving many rotations around the sun and allowing each individual to encounter similarity within the allotted time. In this way, in each lifetime, the individual passes through dimensions again and again. At particular cyclical intervals within certain dimensions there is a similarity, a sense of familiarity to something else which happened before. The individual is experiencing a link with the past at an energy focus point in space where energy principles come together in a very similar way.[1] A vision is a link with the future.

Past, present, and future are a human perspective of an energy sequence.[2]

CONCEPT: A lifetime is a dimension through which different energy passes.[3]

Poem

Passing through.

I will pass through your life.

I appear in human form.
A pattern personified
In physical reality.

As I enter your space
Our patterns connect
In the moments we share
In the cosmic continuum.

I pass through and continue....
You also continue
In a different space,
and in different moments.

No longer together
We continue on Earth
In different dimensions.

The moments we shared
Exist forever.

"I will pass through your life." What does it mean?

The life cycle is a spiral of cosmic energy expression. It is associated with a specific shape—the shape of a natal pattern path which moves with the Earth in a spiral fashion as the Earth rotates. The shape is like a helical coil in which there is relatively more space than coil. As other natal patterns in the same location rotate, they intertwine until the moment of separation. After separation the coils no longer twist around each other. One natal pattern has "passed through" the life cycle of other natal patterns. All the natal patterns continue to spiral.

1. See "Familiarity is a facet of reincarnation." on page 198.
2. See "The Dimensions of Time are like Multiple Window Frames" on page 139.
3. See "Lifetime" on page 169.

CHILDHOOD   YOUTH   MIDLIFE   OLD AGE

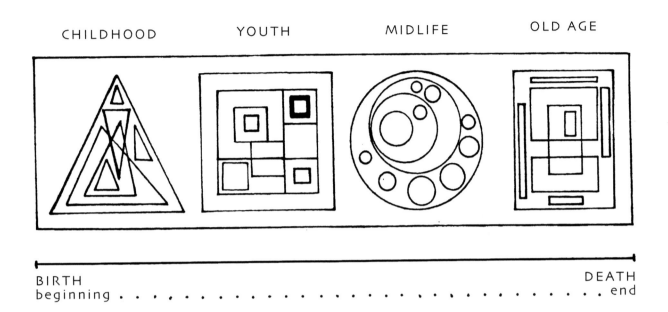

BIRTH
beginning . . . . end

DEATH

Lifetime: Lineal Perception

Most of us think of a lifetime in a lineal way. This illustration shows the various phases in a lifetime in lineal context, where each phase is a moment and all the events of the various phases are contained within such periods. All the moments are contained in one moment—the moment between birth and death.[4] Four simple shapes have been selected to represent four phases of life. Each shape represents a different dimension in each phase.

---

4. See "Time contains all things." on page 110.

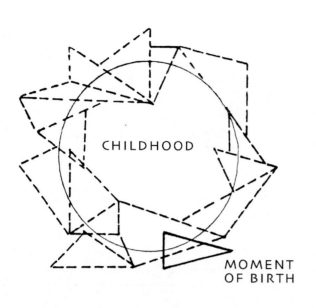

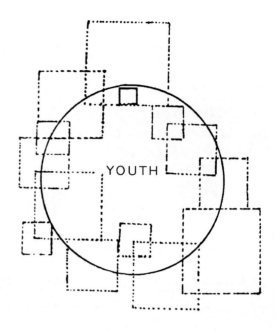

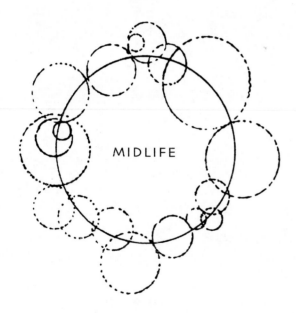

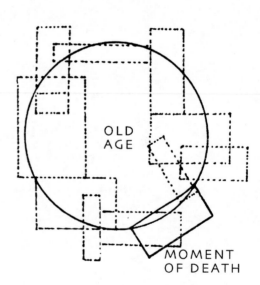

Lifetime: Circular Perception

A lifetime is more accurately depicted in these diagrams.

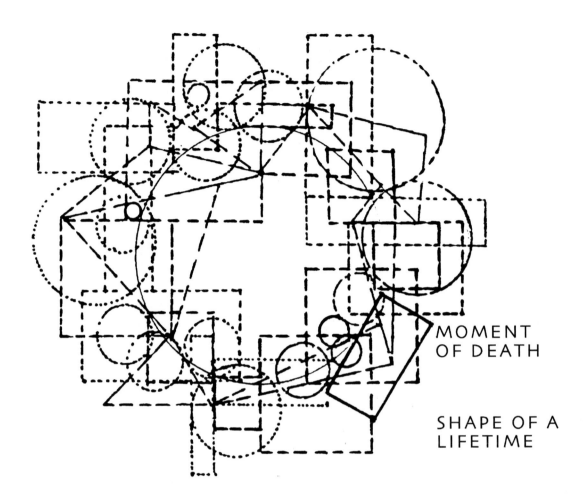

MOMENT
OF DEATH

SHAPE OF A
LIFETIME

Lifetime

A person's lifetime is a collection of dimensions within which all the person's activities are contained and retained as energy imprints.

In symbolic form, the picture of energy looks more like this.

Growing Complexity

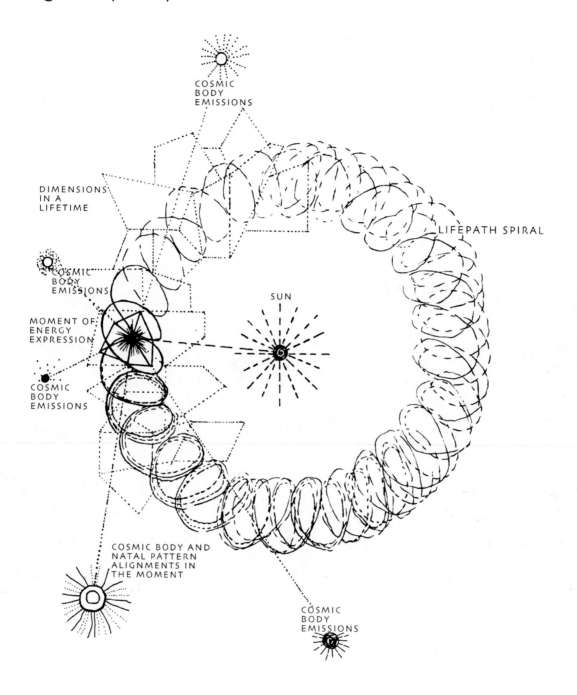

This illustration shows the complexity of shape in a lifetime.

House with Rings Analogy

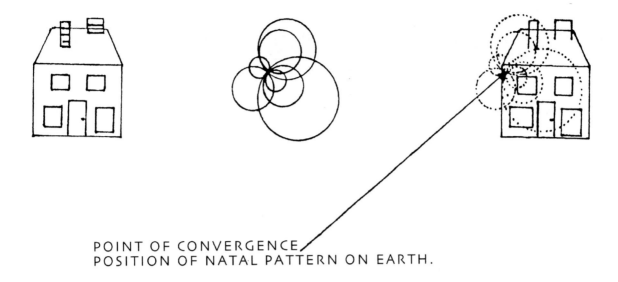

POINT OF CONVERGENCE,
POSITION OF NATAL PATTERN ON EARTH.

The natal position of a natal pattern on Earth is a point of cosmic energy convergence.

In this illustration a lifetime is likened to a house where a collection of rings converge. The house may be interpreted as the sphere of existence in physical reality, or the space in which a lifetime occurs. The rings represent the energy cycles which influence the lifetime according to the natal pattern responses. The point of convergence is a focus point for cosmic energy interaction with the natal pattern.

Energy Impregnation Occurs at the Place of Birth

The arrangement of cosmic forces at the moment of birth is known as the natal pattern.

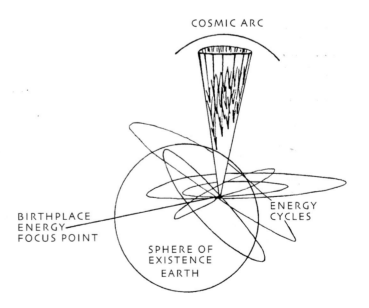

COSMIC ARC

ENERGY
CYCLES

BIRTHPLACE
ENERGY
FOCUS POINT

SPHERE OF
EXISTENCE
EARTH

House with Rings Analogy

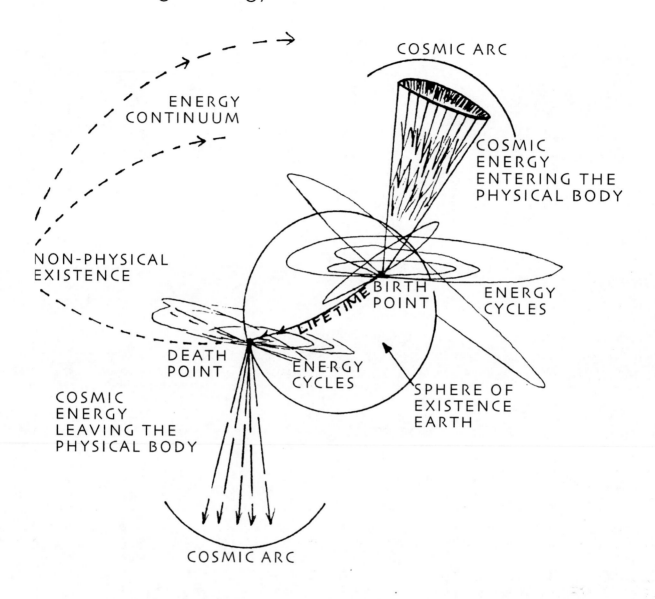

The arrangement of cosmic forces at the moment of death is termed the death pattern. The death position is the energy focus point where physical manifestation changes to non-physical form. The "spirit" (or cosmic energy) circulates in non-physical reality as a soul pattern.[5] Cosmic energy continues to cycle.

CONCEPT: Cosmic energy arrangements are responsible for physical manifestations.[6]

---

5. See "Death Occurs at an Energy Focus Point in Space" on page 182.
6. See "Uniqueness" on page 160.

Existence Cycle

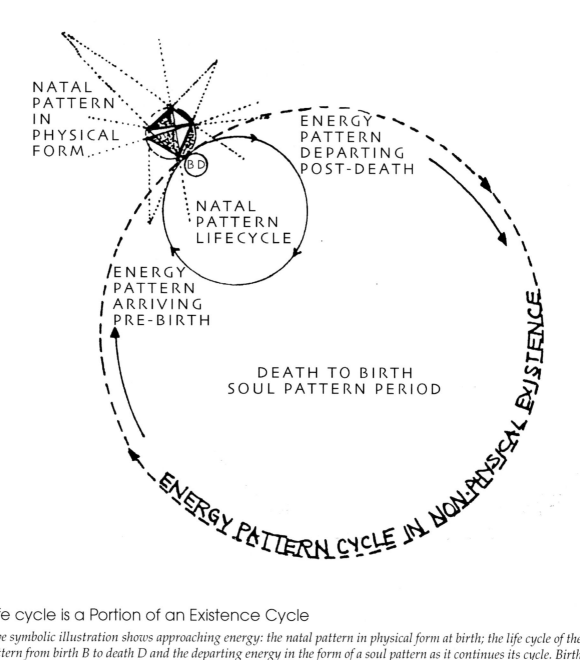

The Life cycle is a Portion of an Existence Cycle

The above symbolic illustration shows approaching energy: the natal pattern in physical form at birth; the life cycle of the natal pattern from birth B to death D and the departing energy in the form of a soul pattern as it continues its cycle. Birth and death are moments which occupy transition points on a cycle which has culminated and declined.

The life cycle is an energy evolvement: a physical, emotional, mental, spiritual, and cultural development.

All cycles are pulses like cosmic heartbeats.
All things obey the universal principle of culmination and decline.

Human Existence: Perspective

Human existence is part of an energy continuum.

We limit ourselves in our concept of existence. By thinking of existence as the period between birth and death does not allow for the depth of understanding which is possible once these limits are removed. It is analogous to the consideration of hydrogen oxide in only one state, invisible steam, and all the beauty of ice forms remain unknown.

HYDROGEN OXIDE

Focus Point BIRTH* ———————— LIFETIME ———————— Focus Point *DEATH

Ice Forms	Water Forms	Vapor Forms
Iceberg	Mist	Water Vapor
Ice cube	Fog	
Icicle	Clouds	
Ice Crystal	Dew	
Snow	Raindrops	
Snowflake		
Frost		
Hail		
Arctic Fog	Steam	
Glacier	River	

Death is a transition, like a change in state.[7]

---

7. See "Death Occurs at an Energy Focus Point in Space" on page 182.

Pisces/Aries Analogy

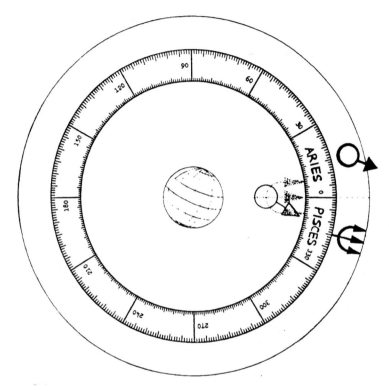

There is No Beginning or Ending, Only An Energy Continuum

This concept of continuity is illustrated using the familiar circle of the zodiac where Pisces meets Aries between 359° and 0°.

Pisces: representing the twelfth house and hidden things is ruled by Neptune. Pisces is associated with the feet. The color is violet.

Aries: representing the first house and the physical body is ruled by Mars. Aries is associated with the head. The color is red.

In astrological terms, the essential quality of Neptune is of concealment, that which is hidden, invisible, or not completely revealed. Something unknown always remains— unfathomable, like the depths of the ocean. In circular terms, as Pisces and Aries touch or connect in the zodiac, Neptune meets Mars in the head within the human body. It is an unseen connection within the cranial capacity for, although Mars rules the head, Neptune rules the brain: subconscious activity, dreams, and private thoughts. Through the physical nervous system, the nerve endings of the feet connect with the nerve centers in the brain. In fetal life, the feet touch the head. In the zodiac, Pisces recedes as Aries comes to the fore. Mars emerges. Neptune disappears. In the visible spectrum, violet meets red.

Human Existence

Each lifetime is a portion of an existence cycle.

The cosmos is an energy system in which, at cyclical intervals, different cosmic energy principles link through synchronicity, causing energy to express in a particular way. Most of us think in terms of beginnings or endings, of starts and finishes, of birth and death. Instead, we should substitute focus points, connection, separation, merging or fusion, and think in terms of an energy continuum—a process without beginning or ending. We should consider a lifetime in physical reality as only a portion of a cycle of existence that merges with other cycles and involves much more than a single lifetime.

Humans are familiar with a lifetime, the relatively short portion between birth and death.

CONCEPT: Humans exist in an energy continuum.

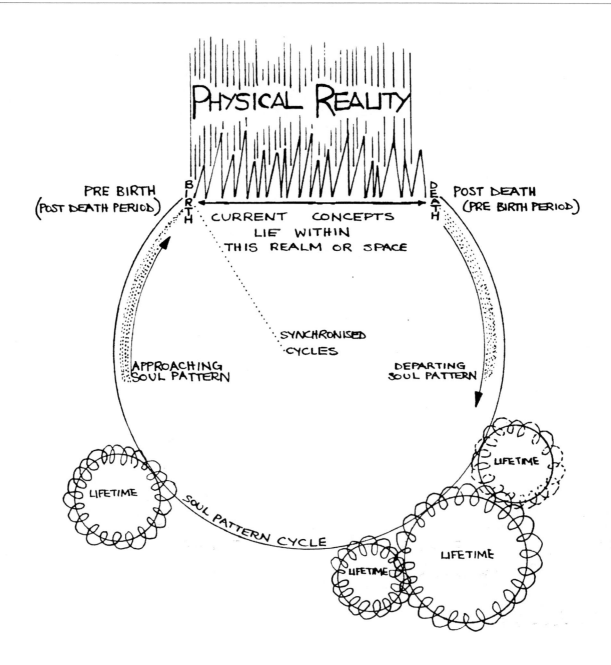

Existence Cycle

This illustration shows a cycle of existence, several energy experiences during a mainly non-physical or discarnate period, and the current lifetime (zig zag) marked between birth and death. The previous lifetimes exist in other dimensions, but are still connected to the existence cycle.

Human Existence: Soul Pattern

The soul is an energy pattern.

A lifetime refers to the portion of human existence in physical reality. As we spiral around the sun, each lifetime is a cyclical rhythm of moments in the dimension of physical reality in which a natal pattern is personified. In the context of an individual as a natal pattern, each human being may be considered a "soul" or "spirit" in physical manifestation. It is the concept of a spirit having a human experience where each individual is the sum of all experiences. The soul is the spirit within. As cosmic energy cycles, recycles and continues to cycle in a continuum of energy exchanges, each human is born, lives, dies, and continues between death and another birth in the form of a soul pattern—a vibration in the cosmos.

CONCEPT: Physical reality is a cosmic energy expression.

Past Lives/Old Souls

Energy patterns evolve in the continuum of cosmic motion.

A lifetime is the expression of a natal pattern in the moment of its physical existence, the moment between birth and death. It represents what happens in a sequence of orbits around the sun. Through multiple rotations, each natal pattern enriches its cosmic energy experience.

Each lifetime is a period of evolving energy in a mosaic of energy movement, a portion of a complex energy pattern cycle within and part of an energy continuum. In each lifetime, each natal pattern is exposed to important energy returns which depend on cyclical intervals and, therefore, span vast cycles and different incarnations.[8] Infrequent cycles cause rare circumstances to come into existence and allow characters to reappear from distant antiquity. As energy patterns reoccur in the cosmos, natal patterns reoccur on Earth—the phenomena of reincarnation and multiple lifetimes exist.[9] Humans are mostly unaware of this, or that everyone is connected to past lives in the present. In this context, a person is not old, in terms of years, but in energy experience. An "old soul" is an energy pattern which has previously existed in physical reality and rotated with the Earth many times.

CONCEPT: Human existence is an evolving process in an energy continuum which acknowledges past lives and old souls.

---

8. See "CONCEPT: Similarity occurs at energy return." on page 80.
9. See "Reincarnation is an energy repetition." on page 194.

METAPHYSICAL CONCEPT: Spiritual evolution occurs by means of energy rearrangement (soul development).

Future Thrust

A lifetime is a potential unit of evolution.

A lifetime is a sequential expression of energy with a future thrust. During each moment, we are each the product of the previous moment of this life and all previous lifetimes. Energy is given to us and extracted from us through the natal pattern, a code for life, which is like a human share of the cosmos.

The individual is a cosmic energy unit in which the thrust is forward. Each unit occupies a position in the system. Complete in itself, it is part of the whole network and is at once necessary. In cosmic terms, humans as energy units cycle; therefore, human expression is cyclical. As cosmic energy comes around again and particular patterns reoccur, humans return, characters reappear.[10] In other words, the individual does not go backwards in life as from old age to childhood. Instead, cosmic energy continues and eventually returns to the same positions in space, familiar dimensions where natal patterns encounter different, yet similar, energy arrangements and create similar though different dimensions. Humans evolve in this way because all patterns contain the Uranian principle which is the agent for change.

In the context of humans as natal patterns, people move through space within moments (shapes defined by energy). Each direction is a unique energy path, determined by the natal pattern. It is experienced alone, regardless of other connections.[11]

In terms of physics, cosmic energy defines space through pattern interaction. The process makes natal patterns evolutionary links. In this way, each lifetime is part of the chain of events in evolution. For each individual, it is the period between birth and death.

Each life evolves; each lifetime is a phase of evolution.

Each lifetime offers a chance for the evolution of energy patterns.

CONCEPTS: Evolution is an energy direction.
Energy patterns evolve as individuals fulfill destiny.
Evolution occurs according to cosmic forces.
Growing complexity.[12]

---

10. See "Energy Return" on page 80; and . "Reincarnation is an energy repetition." on page 194.
11. See "Poem" on page 166.
12. See "Growing Complexity" on page 170.

Fifteen • Death

Acceptance

> *"The bones of the skeleton which support the body can become
> the bars of the cage which imprison the spirit."*
>
> R. Ruth Gendler
> *The Book of Qualities*

Death is part of existence.

There is a time to die, yet society is reluctant to allow death. Instead, society attempts to prolong lives which are ready to change into another form of existence. Everything is done to prevent dying, which creates a burden that is difficult to bear. Death still occurs.

Birth is easily accepted as a part of life, in contrast to death, for which a reason must be found. Death is diagnosed because society is curious about death and insists on knowing the cause of it. In most cases it is written in medical terminology, but understood in lay terms: heart failure, stroke, accident. It is seldom stated in astrological terms. When and how death occurs is determined by the natal pattern response to a particular cosmic configuration, a precise moment when cycles bring an arrangement of energy into existence which has such an extreme effect on the natal pattern that the individual can no longer continue in physical reality and dies.

Throughout life, death is an ever-present possibility, yet modern society is reluctant to accept it. That this feeling exists is exemplified in the numerous discussions which occur following death, particularly unexpected, unusual, or highly publicized deaths. The usual reaction is of dismay, followed by much discussion over a considerable period. Amid the facts and sympathy is the underlying reluctance to accept death as a part of existence. Many try to learn facts from death so that future deaths may be avoided. How futile this appears from a cosmic perspective. It is like a myth that one might live forever. In the acceptance of death is the opportunity to comprehend the meaning of life and to consider the deeper meaning of existence.

Perhaps it is time to acknowledge physical existence as part of something greater than one lifetime.

CONCEPT: Death occurs at an energy focus point in space. Death is a transition, like a change of state.[1]

---

1. See "Hydrogen Oxide," p. 174.

The little girl who died in her mother's arms asked to die naturally because she did not want any more tubes or surgery. The little girl was paving the way for a new age, a time when we will no longer regard death as final, but as a transition between different realities. Knowledge of "the other side," as the spiritual world is often called, will change our understanding of non-physical existence. The little girl may well have been an old soul, someone who was unafraid of death simply because she knew the other side.

Perspective

Birth and death are energy focus points.

At birth the individual is imprinted with a cosmic energy arrangement (the natal pattern). At death, that pattern is released. In this context, birth is an energy capture and death is an energy release.[2]

Cosmic birth includes the inception of a new society, the inauguration of a president, buying new shoes. Cosmic death includes the finality of a demolished building, the fall of an empire, or the death of the countryside when a city is built over the ground.

In cosmic terms, birth and death are transition points in an energy continuum. Death is merely a point on a cycle, a position in space, a moment of particular significance to the individual in which energy leaves the physical body.

Deathpoints which coincide represent mass death. When a group meets death together, it is a common moment shared by many natal patterns, as in a shoal of fish caught in a trawler's net, a city devastated by a large earthquake, or acres of trees in a forest fire.

Wheel Analogy

All life is cyclical, a continuum, like a circle. There is no beginning or ending. Energy merely moves on, like a turning wheel which at one point embraces the ground and the next whizzes through the air. Only one point makes contact at any particular time; the rest of the wheel is at different levels of elevation above the ground. Most of the wheel is out of contact for most of the time, yet every point touches the ground in each revolution.

Birth and death are analogous to the contact points, which are brief and necessary but only positions on a wheel.

Life is associated with cyclical movement: the rotation of the Earth about its axis, the revolution of the Earth around the sun, the revolution of the moon around the Earth. Within this movement, each individual is associated with an invisible circle, an unseen clock face calibrated with cosmic body positions, like a personal circle of the zodiac. Cosmic bodies continue to make their way around. It may be visualized as an electronic game which lights up when connections are made. When particular lights are on, the game is over. Afterwards, another game is possible.[3] Death occurs in the same way, after which another life is possible.

---

2. See "Death Occurs at an Energy Focus Point in Space" on page 182.
3. See "The Life cycle is a Portion of an Existence Cycle" on page 173.

CONCEPT: Life is associated with invisible cycles from which there is no escape.

Continuum

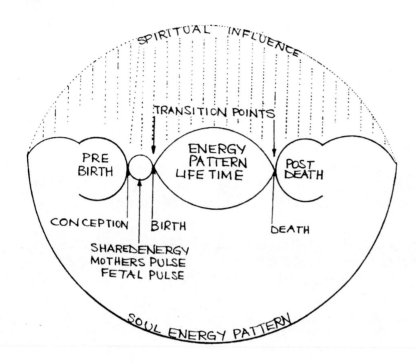

Death Occurs at an Energy Focus Point in Space

This diagram shows an existence cycle in which a lifetime is a potential unit of human evolution.[4] Within the time frame between death and birth, the residual pattern experiences other lifetimes and much non-physical reality.

CONCEPT: Total existence includes physical and non-physical reality.

METAPHYSICAL CONCEPT: The greater part of existence is in non-physical reality.

Perspective

An energy pattern has the capacity to manifest in physical form under particular conditions. The life process illustrates the conversion of energy into material matter. Without a pattern of energy, life in physical reality does not exist. When a pattern can no longer tolerate the prevailing cosmic energy directions, the physical form dies.[5] The residual energy arrangement, or soul pattern, is released and continues to cycle in non-physical reality. The corpse cannot sustain its form without its energy field and slowly begins to disintegrate. Physical death releases energy for recycling in a more appropriate way.

---

4. Ontogeny recapitulates phylogeny: the stages that a developing embryo goes through (ontogeny) traces the stages that a species has gone through in its evolution (phylogeny).
5. See: page 43, Llewellyn's Calendar, death of Billy Martin, 1991.

The effect of cosmic energy is a cyclical existence for all things, which means that death is not final, but merely a transition from a phase. As energy cycles, another phase occurs in the cosmic energy continuum.

Perhaps death should be considered as a departure from a lifetime than as the end of existence, a transition from physical reality as energy moves on a cycle in another dimension. The energy entry pattern (natal pattern) is different from the energy exit pattern (death pattern). The change is in energy arrangement. The energy expression of a natal pattern in a lifetime is the portion of the evolution which has occurred. With comprehension of this energy process and wise use of the powerful forces available, humans may begin to direct their own evolution.

Cosmic energy is a cyclical continuum.

All things on Earth are cyclical.

Destiny

Everything is initiated and terminated by a cosmic configuration.

Everything on Earth has an energy shape, which is held together by cosmic forces and controlled by a cosmic code. This code is the natal pattern.

When a person is born, the cosmos is arranged in a particular way. Each cosmic body is in a position relative to another and to the Earth. This cosmic energy arrangement determines the natal pattern, the manner of birth, and marks the event for the mother. When a person dies, the cosmos is arranged differently because cosmic bodies have moved. This arrangement brings about the response that determines the death pattern and marks the manner of death. The changes in cosmic body positions indicate a period of cosmic movement. The responses of a natal pattern to this movement are specific expressions of energy, moments which correspond to the shapes or dimensions of a physical lifetime. For this reason each lifetime is a unique experience on Earth.

Humans call this destiny.[6]

---

6. See "Suggested Reading" on page 203.

Sixteen • Destiny

Lifepath

Destiny is an energy direction.

Since antiquity people have pondered over the way everything happens.
When something cannot be explained, it is attributed to fate.

Physics explains energy in technical terms. Fate, which appears to be inexplicable, may be understood through the physics, mathematics, and architecture of cosmic energy which astrology makes lucid. Through the synchronicity of unified energy fields, energy arrangements come into being in a particular momentary sequence—the path of destiny which describes fate. In this way cosmic energy links fate with physics. It is a fascinating connection.

For all of us, why something happens now and not later, why one owns this car and not that one, is directly associated with the natal pattern. Fate is the response of a natal pattern to cosmic energy. It is an energy path controlled by the natal pattern in its relationship to the cosmos. Since each natal pattern is a unique energy unit, the prevailing cosmic arrangement affects each pattern differently. This means that each moment of energy expression is different for each natal pattern. Each natal pattern has its own path. Each path is different. Each destiny is an individual experience.

PRINCIPLE: Cosmic body movement is predictable.

ENERGY EXPRESSION: Natal pattern responses occur in a particular way.

ENERGY EFFECT: Destiny.

CONCEPT: Inevitability.

Everything on Earth responds to cosmic forces,
As a marionette is pulled by particular strings.

Future Thrust

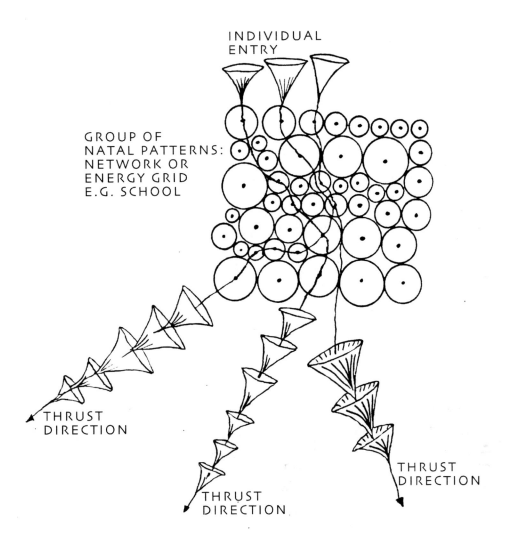

INDIVIDUAL
ENTRY

GROUP OF
NATAL PATTERNS:
NETWORK OR
ENERGY GRID
E.G. SCHOOL

THRUST
DIRECTION

THRUST
DIRECTION

THRUST
DIRECTION

Cosmic Connections Determine Destiny

This diagram shows entry into and movement through a school group. Natal pattern responses and interaction cause energy to thrust in particular directions. Each direction is different. The group allows energy experience and growth. Some groups prevent energy growth.[1]

---

1. See "Circuitry" on page 31.

Karma

The natal pattern determines destiny.

Fate…
Freewill and destiny…
Chance and necessity…
Choice…
Cosmic energy embraces all of these.

Doctrines in the past have leaned heavily in certain directions causing humanity to believe it is all fate, or all free will, when, in fact, energy influences link both together.

Humans are locked into destiny by natal patterns.[2] For each pattern, there is a potential energy expression. In defining the space, the moment determines the boundaries and limits the expression. Thus, a natal pattern both permits and denies choice. In this context, a natal pattern may be likened to a box of chocolates from which a selection is made. The choice is limited by the contents; the order is influenced by the selection. Inevitably, the last chocolate is the final choice and forces a decision.

Human choice exists only within natal pattern potential. Patterns are controlled by cycles, so that choices exist at certain times within this energy framework. Sometimes there is no choice when the influence of Saturn forces a direction in life. Free will occurs through Uranian energy, the influence within the universe which causes change and the precursor of evolution. Chance and necessity also involve the influence of Jupiter, and work together in a complementary way. Having been given a chance (Jupiter/Uranus), necessity (Saturn) often influences the next decision. Having made the decision, another chance often presents itself. Thus, a direction occurs which fulfills destiny and is part of karma.

---

2. See "CONCEPT: Life is associated with invisible cycles from which there is no escape." on page 182.

Destiny is linked to karma through Saturn in the natal pattern.

There is an old saying that implies the teacher arrives when the student is ready. We meet the people we are meant to meet, at a certain time and for a particular reason. Through Saturn, the karmic planet, the energy principle which teaches and disciplines, destiny puts people and events together for karmic purposes. Encounters are perfectly synchronized energy connections because everything which occurs is energy related. In this way, only certain encounters are ever made. They may be described as destined.[3][4][5]

Destiny is the response of a natal pattern to cosmic forces.
What happens determines our fate on Earth.[6]

A profound change will occur when humans decide to choose natal patterns.

3. See "Cosmic Links" on page 23.
4. See "Saturn" on page 61.
5. See "Everything is in separate dimensions." on page 129.
6. See "The Universal Excuse" on page 155.

Seventeen • Karma

Perspective

Many things which seem inexplicable
are best explained by considering a far greater reality.

"In Buddhism, the sum of a person's actions in one of his successive states of
existence, regarded as determining his fate in the next; hence, necessary fate or destiny,
following as effect from cause. Hence Karmic a."

The Shorter Oxford English Dictionary
Volume 1 A-M reprinted 1959

In some belief systems, karma is the term for the reason why a person has a particular fate.[1] It is "based on the concept that deeds determine destiny, so that an individual is rewarded, or punished relative to past actions."[2] In this sense, karma is an interpretation of destiny.

"Whatsoever a man soweth that shall he also reap" (Galatians 6:7) exemplifies a similar theme. This ancient observation of a universal principle of balance illustrates that human life is not exempt from cosmic laws.

In this book karma is presented in terms of cosmic energy.

CONCEPT: Karma is an energy phenomenon.

Equilibrium

Karma is an energy equilibrium

Karma is like an unwritten law of energy balance between polarities, which extends beyond simple cycles and, therefore, one lifetime. It is observed as an equilibrium. Cosmic energy conforms to the nature of energy which moves between poles, and acknowledges the principle of balance between extremes. In the continuum of cosmic processes, the nature of energy movement insists on eventual balance. Known as cosmic justice, karma exists because of cosmic energy cycles. Karma continues because all cosmic bodies are represented in every natal pattern. In this way, cycles allow karma to resolve itself as energy comes around again and patterns return, even from distant antiquity.

---

1. Karma, see Glossary, page 211.
2. See "Suggested Reading," *Larousse Encyclopedia of Astrology*, on page 203.

Karma is often observed in everyday life, but may not be concerned with energy behavior, in particular cosmic energy principles. For instance, generosity and greed are positive and negative effects of Jupiter: the planet of benevolence. When people decide to reduce expenditure by denying others, in order to have more money for themselves, the decision usually leads to a greater cost to them in the long run. In contrast, unselfish generosity is inundated with gifts, as though the cosmos rushes in to fill a vacuum. The emptier a space becomes through giving, the more room there is to accept what is given, and very often, what arrives is more appropriate. The cosmic issue here is that one cannot continue to take without giving. As the world in general takes from the Earth without replenishment, so the masses of an impoverished Earth suffer the consequences. Ultimately, no one is spared.[3]

Thus, from a cosmic perspective, we need to consider ourselves in terms of a relationship to everything else—one energy pattern among all the others. This is fundamental to the unity among all things.

All things are energy arrangements. All things conform to the laws of cosmic energy.

Energy Reversal

Karma is considered in terms of Uranus.

Uranus causes change through sudden upset by turning things around or upside down and by reversal. Karma is a manifestation of energy reversal which occurs when Uranus gives energy expression a twist.

In terms of cosmic energy, karma is linked to energy return. In the continuum of the cosmos, energy arrangements are similar at cyclical intervals. When these moments are influenced by Uranus, conditions, events, and characters are seemingly in reverse.[4] Geophysical processes of erosion, sedimentation, and upheaval give evidence that mountain peaks wear down to disappear beneath the sea, and ocean floors are raised to form lofty peaks once more. That this happens over and over again illustrates the continuum of our cosmic energy heritage.

Greed, cruelty, and arrogance are personality traits dependent on energy principles within the natal pattern.[5] In human affairs, enormous greed is often followed by a devastating loss: cruelty experiences torture; the haughty suffer humility. Karma appears to be punishing. It is the observable outcome of a cosmic energy effect which suggests that a balance eventually occurs.

3. See "Neptune's Revenge" on page 67.
4. See "Dissimilarity obscures energy return." on page 86.
5. See: "Suggested Reading," *The Book of Qualities,* Ruth Gendler, on page 203.

Cyclical Influence

Karmic links are energy links.

In terms of a natal pattern, the individual is linked to other dimensions through the cyclical nature of cosmic energy. Vast cycles are involved. In this way, the natal pattern link with prevailing cosmic patterns involves far more than present life challenges.

Each cycle of Saturn is approximately 29 years. When this cycle is associated with one, or more, very slowly moving cosmic bodies, such as Neptune or Pluto, the cyclical interval is extended considerably, so that a complex cycle may span hundreds or thousands of years. Although it may be mind boggling to realize that an energy influence might have an effect over such immense periods, nevertheless the cycles exist and natal patterns, being part of the system, are connected with them.

Dimension overlay is the feature of energy return which reveals karma. As cycles return energy, the energy shapes of moments in the present exhibit much similarity to the shapes of particular dimensions from the past. Frequent cycles return conditions reminiscent of colonial settlement or the stock market crash. Infrequent cycles cause conditions that once existed in antiquity: Atlantis, ancient Greece, or Peru. In this way karma continues, even after thousands of years and reflects the cyclical movement of cosmic bodies.[6] In this context, karma is an effect of energy return and an interpretation of cosmic influences.[7]

Karmic Recoding

Karma influences destiny.

It is a human trait to be so concerned with mundane matters and personal needs that the cosmic picture is often overlooked. Events happen and pass. Destinies are interwoven. People come together and separate, yet remain linked through cosmic energy, for everything is connected in a rhythm of energy cycles. Everything in the present is linked to the past.

We are all influenced by the direction from which we have come. The path to the present moment is the background experience with which we connect, and from which we draw in order to cope with the present. Our past is the precursor of our future.[8] A turning point is reached at times of introspection. Thus, re-evaluation is often in the wake of a significant event which is, in itself, a harbinger of change. This often coincides with a change in destiny, a time of changing energy arrangements which are the pre-requisite of evolution: physical, emotional, mental, and spiritual, all of which is reflected in soul development and cultures. In a time of karmic recoding, lifestyle patterns are re-arranged as coinciding energy cycles influence a new direction.

---

6. See "Suggested Reading," *Astrological Timing* by Dane Rudhyar, on page 203; and Black Monday, 1929 and Black Friday, October, 1987.
7. See "Dissimilarity obscures energy return." on page 86; and "CONCEPT: Similarity occurs at energy return." on page 80.
8. See "CONCEPT: The past pervades the present." on page 138.

Karmic bonds involve familiar patterns.

All cosmic interaction begins with an energy connection.[9] In each karmic encounter, each of us easily lapses into an established mode or past-life pattern, because there is familiarity with the energy arrangement. In the release of karmic ties, the bond with another pattern needs to be broken. For the individual, it may be a catastrophic experience. Life changes forever so that karmic recoding may seem to be a period of disruption. It is merely a change in order for destiny to fulfill itself. In this it is very important.

When particular soul patterns are synchronised during several lifetimes, physical reality allows karmic ties to be worked out together. Natal patterns, which have strong karmic links, often reappear at the same time under different circumstances and, once again, become involved in a relationship through pattern connection until the karmic link is released. Thus, it is possible to meet "someone" from the distant past and to reconnect with them in this lifetime to complete or continue karma. Due to the influence of the Uranian cycle, some reversal of conditions is usually evident, such as a devoted husband and wife having been master and slave.

In each lifetime, each karmic encounter is resolved, unresolved, changed to be completed, or continued during another lifetime.

Saturn

Saturn controls karmic encounters.

In its response to the cosmos, each natal pattern creates the moments of its existence in physical reality through changing links with cosmic bodies. These individual moments link the lifepath together. From time to time, certain spaces must be shared with other natal patterns. Energy expression is determined by the combination of energy links which create the structure of the moment. These shapes are shared moments in which one natal pattern passes through the lifepath of another. The nature of the moments depends on the combination of energy influences. Moments shared with natal patterns of significance to the individual are a part of karma. The patterns may be people, pets, or material possessions.

The moments of a lifetime are much influenced by karma, so that a lifetime is often considered to be a learning experience, an opportunity, not only to gain wisdom, but also repay debts, reap rewards, and collect dues. Therefore, even though a very long period elapses, circumstances will occur which offer a chance for karmic dues. These moments are significant in each lifepath. The range is from fortunate connections and favorable expression (the wonderful life) to the reverse: a miserable life, a mere existence due to a very difficult karma, epitomized in the phrase: "It will come back to haunt you."

---

9. See "Everything is initiated and terminated by a cosmic configuration." on page 183.

Perspective

Karmic encounters are brought about by Saturn so that karmic connections usually take the form of a teaching/learning experience, in which the natal patterns involved are forced to come to terms with particular issues. Personified, Saturn is like a hard taskmaster.[10] When personal wishes seem thwarted, the individual feels restricted (Saturn), or controlled in some way, even led as though placed by unseen forces. In reality, the natal pattern is moving in a particular direction which often becomes apparent upon reflection. Everything is the way it is because nothing happens by chance; everything is a cosmic energy interaction.[11]

All strong karmic connections are very profound associations, so that in a karmic sense, people are brought together for a reason. In some karmic encounters, two individuals may have been very favorably and well connected during previous incarnations. They appear again for mutual love and support, rather like helping each other out. In other karmic encounters, much energy imbalance exists. It is usually a reflection of a previous life in which one pattern dominated or hurt another in some way. At first, the patterns tend to interact as before, like lapsing into the way it used to be—old habits, familiar ways. The issues need to be resolved and the patterns released from their karmic bondage. These encounters are often serious experiences.

The difference between leaving someone and having someone removed from one, either through death or departure, is in the karmic process. The result is the same: separation, which by choice and not force, means individuals choose to release each other. Karma usually offers a choice before finally forcing the issue.

Death is cosmic intervention without choice.

10. See "Saturn forces natal patterns to learn." on page 62.
11. See "CONCEPT: Inevitability." on page 52.

The Influence of Staturn: The Timer

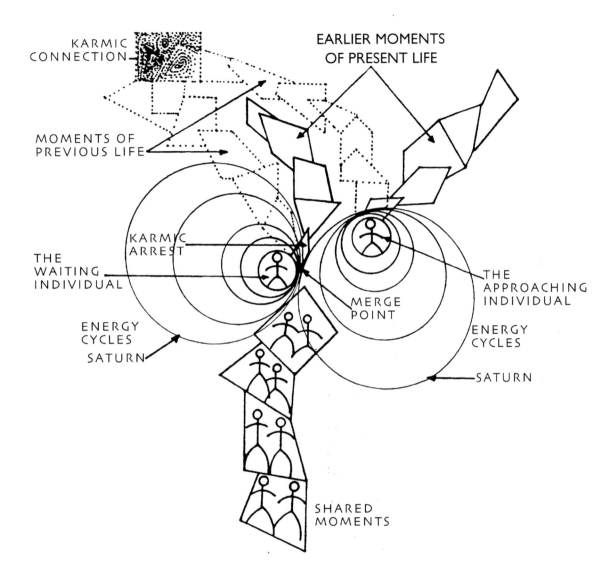

KARMIC
CONNECTION

EARLIER MOMENTS
OF PRESENT LIFE

MOMENTS OF
PREVIOUS LIFE

KARMIC
ARREST

THE
WAITING
INDIVIDUAL

THE
APPROACHING
INDIVIDUAL

MERGE
POINT

ENERGY
CYCLES

ENERGY
CYCLES

SATURN

SATURN

SHARED
MOMENTS

This is a symbolic illustration of an encounter involving important karmic ties. The diagram shows the point of karmic arrest through the controlling influence of Saturn, in order for the patterns (individuals) to synchronize for connection.

Eighteen • Reincarnation

Cosmic Similarity

Reincarnation is an energy repetition.

The cyclical movement of cosmic bodies permits energy patterns to reoccur. Like old codes being recirculated, energy pattern repetition offers an interpretation of, and lends credence to, reincarnation.

The concept of reincarnation in terms of energy patterns, which from time to time return to particular positions on Earth, is based on two principles: specificity and similarity. Each cosmic body causes a particular influence and, therefore, has a specific effect. Similar configurations cause similar influences. Through cosmic movement, cosmic energy continues after the event it caused has passed, and returns to repeat its influence, again and again, creating similar occurrences. Similarity is observed at energy return, which at cyclical intervals insists on similar, though not necessarily identical, cosmic energy expression causing similar moments and similar events on Earth.

In the study of astrology, it is impossible to remain unaware of the vastness of cosmic body cycles and, therefore, energy links with antiquity through these cycles. Within this cosmic continuum, there are historical parallels as energy patterns repeat. Similar characters reappear and similar things happen again and again. In this context, reincarnation is not only possible but probable; we return in another guise.

Foxgloves

Reincarnation may be interpreted in the same way that the foxgloves return.

Each year the foxgloves return. The leaves return, the flowers reappear when they should and as they should, again and again. They are not the same leaves or flowers, but an energy expression of genes within the cosmos. They follow the same genetic code which represents a pattern of energy. Year after year, they return faithfully as the seasons pass, and seem the same. Energy is trapped in the foxglove seeds and conforms to a pattern—the gene pattern. It is a residual energy pattern, a code that connects with a cycle. The gene pattern is like a memory; the memory is always in the seed, but only cosmic interaction allows the foxgloves to appear.

Cosmic Permission

Genes are like memories in physical form.

Genes are accepted as the units of inherited characteristics, or what is fused into a new life at conception.

During the period of embryonic and fetal life, physical development occurs in such a way that birth reveals what is generally observed as particular inherited traits. As growth and development continue, likenesses become more or less easily recognized, allowing identification with certain familial characteristics. Particular offspring favor particular relatives. Even though a gene is not apparent in first generations of offspring, the evidence of its existence is observed, sometimes several generations later. Some traits may seem to have disappeared.

When genes are passed on, the selection is like a box of crayons in which the colors are limited—only some colors are available. What is inherited is like a package. What is fused into the continuum of physical life does not always manifest, indicating that not all inherited characteristics appear in subsequent lineage. What does appear and is, therefore, seen to be a familial trait, depends more on the cosmic energy influence than may be apparent.[1]

Children often closely resemble great-grandparents more than parents or grandparents. This suggests that cycles influence the traits which manifest in physical life at particular intervals. Links with these intervals, such as Saturn's cycle of approximately 29 years, indicate that energy cycles play an important part and influence physical life as well as genes.[2] That a trait manifests at all has much more to do with cosmic permission, or the influence of prevailing forces at birth (which determines the natal pattern) than which genes are inherited in the new physical being. In other words, cosmic energy determines which genes will be expressed.

CONCEPT: Gene expression, like everything else, depends on cosmic permission.

Memory

Memories exist in different forms.

Reincarnation occurs in the way that a familial trait continues and reappears. A gene manifests according to cosmic permission; it is cycle linked. A gene is a memory. Reincarnation, like a gene in physical reality, is also a memory—the name for the repetition of a cosmic energy pattern. It could be argued that this is not so, that energy patterns merely repeat causing similar circumstances. However, humans experience familiarity indicative of memory.[3]

Although memories exist, only the cosmos permits access, or recall, which is an effect of cosmic energy expression. Reincarnation as an effect of cosmic energy expression is a very

1. See *Neptune in Focus,* forthcoming from the author.
2. See "Suggested Reading," *The Forces of Destiny,* Penny Thornton, on page 203.
3. See *Neptune in Focus,* forthcoming from the author.

similar phenomenon to the gene memory. As a natal pattern is repeated, a memory is also recovered, as data is stored in and may be recovered from a computer. Past-life memories are recovered in a similar way, access depends on alignments.

CONCEPT: Reincarnation is the cosmic energy expression of a memory.

Interpretation

Reincarnation is not well understood. By definition, it is existence in the flesh again. In terms of physics, life is energy in a particular form: human, animal, plant. Reincarnation refers to life which has experienced physical life in a previous time. In terms of cosmic energy, reincarnation may be considered from a different perspective.

The human person does not return again. It is an energy pattern which returns and personifies an individual in similar physical manifestation who remembers and is familiar with another lifetime.

Some energy patterns linked to short cycles such as the yearly cycle, manifest frequently, like the foxgloves, which reappear, or new mushrooms which pop up quickly, as if from nowhere. They are not the same flowers or the same mushrooms, but exhibit similarities. Energy patterns linked to less frequent cycles may not be observed as easily but still occur.

All connections are cosmic energy connections. This means that human relationships extend beyond a single lifetime because connections are linked to energy cycles. In this way humans are also linked with energy cycles and "return": cyclical patterns with access to memories, but they are

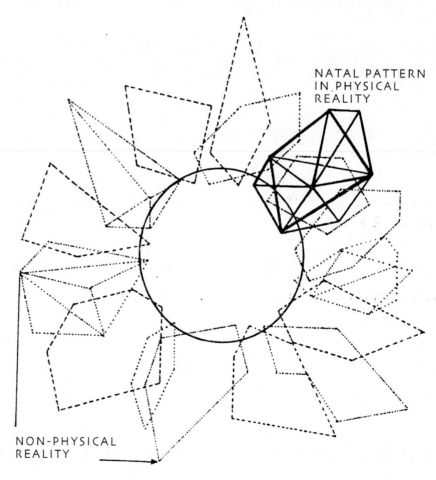

NATAL PATTERN IN PHYSICAL REALITY

NON-PHYSICAL REALITY

not the same people. Someone who reincarnates is not a person returned from the dead, but a natal pattern that is very similar to a previous pattern, a code through which memory or particular memories may be retrieved. Access to these memories may seem as though we have lived before.

Soul Memory

Reincarnation is a memory with a haunting familiarity.

Reincarnation is an energy phenomenon, a feature of the sixth dimension which links the present with the dimensions of another time. It occurs through energy pattern repetition and embraces vast cycles of cosmic body relationships spanning millennia. It is a feature of energy return.

It is suggested that some individuals contain within themselves memories of people who have lived before. The link with previous lives is through cosmic energy by means of soul-memory access. Humans do not live again in terms of the same individuals, but rather in the ability of the mind to access the soul memory and, thus, be familiar with previous lives.

Each individual represents an energy pattern. Each lifetime represents the moments of an energy pattern path (destiny). The concept is that even though multitudes of people have existed before us, the moments of their lives remain in the specific dimensions of their existence. Particular cosmic links allow access to the memory of previous lives in the same way that individuals recall memories of the present life. By accessing those dimensions, it is possible to know about those lives and to recover wisdom and knowledge.[4]

From time to time in the cosmos, extremely similar cosmic configurations exist giving rise to extremely similar natal patterns. These patterns, like identical twins, allow identical people to live at different times. When this happens, the similarity of each moment in a destined path, facilitates recognition of past dimensions through a similarity of energy shapes. Reincarnates easily connect with previous lives and sense familiarity.

In this interpretation of reincarnation, a particular energy pattern once again occurs in human form as a very similar cosmic energy arrangement reoccurs. Reincarnation may be considered in terms of a vibration that exists, which allows soul-memory access through the repetition of an energy pattern. This is what is meant by reincarnation.

CONCEPT: Reincarnation is a facet of memory.

This illustration shows the crystalline concept of a natal pattern in a single moment in physical reality and the dimensions of non-physical reality (sensitive energy shapes). All are linked in the cycles of energy continuum.

The dimension of physical reality with which humans are the most familiar is a portion of total existence. Each moment in each lifetime is like a fragment of a thread in the fabric of the cosmic loom.

4. See *Neptune in Focus,* forthcoming from the author.

Physical Manifestation

Soul Memory

Reincarnation is linked with soul memory.

Each Earth life is lived out, complete in itself, according to the natal pattern expression. It is the spirit, or soul pattern, which "reincarnates." In metaphysical concept, it is a spirit having a human experience, an energy arrangement experiencing physical reality.

During physical manifestation, a soul reincarnates exactly when a cosmic energy arrangement permits entry into the physical world. At the focus point of birth, another physical experience begins. That soul (spirit) will not leave physical reality until a cosmic energy arrangement once again permits death. At this time the natal pattern has fulfilled its destiny and is released from the physical limits of earthly life.[5]

In the perpetual cosmic energy flux, the various patterns exist in physical and non-physical form. Within this energy framework, the soul memory remains intact, like the genes that simply know what to do.

The soul is an energy pattern.

Each natal pattern contains the soul memory like an energy heritage. The information has always been there, only the process of recall needs to be awakened. Even in the present lifetime, all that remains are our memories. As we lose the ability to recall and remember, we forget earlier life. Whether it is in this life, or past lives, the energy process is the same.

Soul-memory access is not always a conscious endeavor. It is frequently a familiarity with an "unknown" place or person, with natural skills or knowledge. It ranges from a vague stirring within the mind to a well-developed awareness of a past life. Soul-memory access is the method for bringing important and relevant information from the past. Vivid memory recall allows knowledge and wisdom to be brought into the current moment for use.

Acknowledgment of this memory assists ability in its access, which is usually easier with a medium. Soul-memory access is distinct from channeled information which is received from entities.[6]

It is time to awaken our energy heritage, to access the memories of past lives.

Haunting Familiarity

Familiarity is a facet of reincarnation.

The human experience of reincarnation is a haunting familiarity.

A lifetime is like a crystalline corridor through which cosmic energy continually passes.[7] When particular natal patterns meet within certain shapes, the moments of their

---

5. Saturn (limitation; restriction; Kronos the timer in the zodiac) is always involved with death and karma.
6. See "Suggested Reading," Kathryn Ridall, on page 203.
7. See "Dimensions Are Like Crystals" on page 136.

interaction trigger a memory. There is a feeling of familiarity as previous dimensions are accessed.

Dimensions may be likened to rooms within buildings. Just as we frequent our own living room, or visit places in which others have been, such as a pub or cinema, cosmic energy enters and passes through dimensions. In this way, dimensions are like invisible shapes which are re-entered continually as energy moves through their space. Most natal patterns pass through dimensions without connection. When a natal pattern passes through a familiar dimension, energy recognition causes reconnection with the structural imprint (energy-sensitive shape). The human experience is a haunting familiarity with certain places, people, and things. It is like an attachment to a favorite chair or corner of a room in which we feel comfortable, or for no apparent reason, the dislike of an old house that we are only too ready to leave.

CONCEPT: Memory is triggered when cosmic energy recognizes shape.

The Ghosts of Destiny

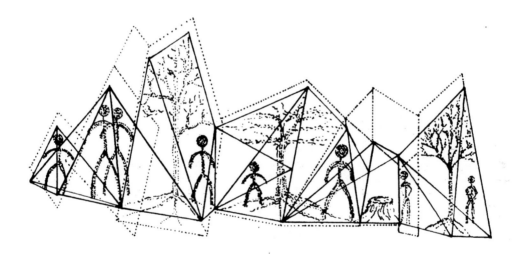

While moments form through natal pattern cosmic interaction, dimensions remain as energy imprints, like a residual energy path. These invisible energy shapes which allow a haunting familiarity when natal patterns pass through them are like ghosts of destiny.[8]

8. See "Crystalline Corridor" on page 136.

Reversed Roles

Theatrical Analogy

Reincarnation helps to explain karmic links.

Reincarnation occurs through the cyclical nature of cosmic energy; similar characters appear in different lifetimes. Different incarnations vary because the Uranian principle changes the expression of the energy arrangement. For this reason roles differ and are often observed to be reversed at different cyclical intervals. This allows energy balance, observed as karma, through the dual nature of the universe, or the polarity of cosmic energy.

Consider a theatrical group, and performances in which each player is always cast in a particular role, so that the audience begins to identify each player with a certain type of character. Then consider a series of plays in which the same group of actors appear in different roles: the actor who always portrayed the familiar father figure, whom we have all grown to love so much, is now the villain of the piece; the lover is now a young child; and the coward now plays a handsome and courageous hero. Each play is different, yet there is a familiarity because the cast is the same. Only the roles are differently assigned as each player learns how to portray different characters.[9] The audience needs to accept the new roles in the same way that we need to accept change in our lives on Earth.

In essence, a play is an arrangement of cosmic energy in space and identifies a moment in the cosmos. Different performances are different moments of energy expression or arrangements of energy.

Musings

Old souls are natal patterns associated with many previous incarnations, like actors who are associated with numerous different performances. When one ponders that one may have been on Earth before, perhaps many times in many different forms, each lifetime is like another visit. Patience may have been learned as a tree in a forest.

Reincarnation is the repetition of an energy pattern.
The natal pattern is the linking factor.

---

9. Reversed roles illustrate an energy effect of Uranus which tends to turn things around. See "Uranus turns things around." on page 63, "Similarity" on page 81; and "Character appearance is a cyclical phenomenon." on page 85.

Nineteen • Cosmic Conclusion

Perspective

Within the cosmos all things happen, and pass.

The mountains bask in the sunshine. They have existed for a long time and witnessed hordes of humans pass by. From a human perspective, it would seem that the mountains have always been there. From a cosmic perspective, they have not. They came into physical existence as an effect of cosmic energy, huge Earth upheavals a very long time ago. The energy which is manifested in mountains is the same as the energy which is manifested in humans. Only the arrangement is different. The cycles which brought energy patterns together to form mountains are infrequent. In the same way, infrequent cycles bring energy patterns together from distant antiquity and allow knowledge from the past.

Fleeting individuality exists in an infinite energy continuum, a vastness of energy cycles in which the momentary nature of a human lifetime is a unique expression of energy on Earth. Reincarnation, in terms of cosmic similarity, expands the dimension of existence and gives it a deeper meaning. Physical reality is enriched with non-physical overtones. The feeling of belonging to the universe strengthens. Everything must be considered and included; nothing is separate from the whole. Everything is linked. Everything participates and contributes. Everything in the cosmos affects everything else. Destinies are interwoven. It is in this context that we should regard ourselves.

CONCEPT: Individual energy is part of cosmic energy.

Enlightenment

Humans are poised in the dawn of a new age.

The Uranus-Neptune conjunction created a chance for a spiritual reawakening. Through cognition and understanding, humans are becoming more aware of their place in the cosmic whole, and beginning to realize that everything shares the same energy, but in different ways and expresses it differently. These differences, which account for a richness in diversity among all things, including human individuality, allow evolution through the principle of uniqueness. As spiritual awareness grows, and humans increasingly comprehend the universal energy system, the emphasis will focus on wisdom and a wish to learn from the past, through soul-memory access and channels. Understanding the processes within the cosmos is fundamental to the change in human destiny. It is essential to use this knowledge wisely.

People are the way they are, and most do things without knowledge of the underlying processes. We may think we make the decisions about what we do, such as going for a walk or learning to dance, but, in reality, energy takes us into each moment and into destiny. Intermittently, we have choices, therefore, these moments are very critical and important.

Creating new patterns of thinking for a new age is humanity's greatest challenge at the present time. Once again evolution will occur through the human mind, a change in brain use, thinking, and attitudes. Destiny could become a human choice.

Cosmic Indifference

Cosmic energy depends on configuration.

Cosmic energy is ubiquitous—an unseen presence which constantly influences our lives. It is responsible for all things and everything which happens in a continuing relationship between the cosmos and Earth. Cosmic relationships affect human relationships. Understanding the human link with the cosmos is through astrology. As bodies in the cosmos change position, energy influences change. The effect causes humans to change on Earth. Energy patterns evolve in the flux.

As the Earth spins and travels around the sun, the cosmos rearranges itself in a continuum of energy movement. In their orbits, the planets align and sweep past, indifferent, for power is neutral, yet everything is affected. All things are caught in this motion—trapped, like the tiny colored shapes in a rotating kaleidoscope. The individual is also an energy shape moving with the Earth, a natal pattern controlled by its own arrangement. Like pieces in a game of chess, natal patterns move in particular ways. In this is an acceptance of ourselves—our limitations, our potential, and, ultimately, our place in the cosmos.

It is time then to comprehend cosmic energy and everything it embraces.

It is time to acknowledge the essential pattern.

Suggested Reading

Brau, Jean-Louis, Helen Weaver, and Allan Edmands. *Larousse Encyclopedia of Astrology*. NY: McGraw-Hill, 1980.

Bullis, Douglas. *Crystals: The Science, Mysteries and Lore*. New York: Friedman Group, 1990.

Ebertin, Reinhold. *The Combination of Stellar Influences*. trans. Alfred G. Roosedale and Linda Kratzsch. Tempe, AZ: American Federation of Astrologers, 1994.

Gendler, J. Ruth. *The Book of Qualities*. NY: Perennial Library, 1988.

Hall, Manley P. *Astrological Keywords*.

Hand, Robert. *Planets in Transit: Life Cycles for Living*. Gloucester, MA: Para Research, 1976.

Hand Clow, Barbara. *Chiron: Rainbow Bridge Between the Inner and Outer Planets*. St. Paul: Llewellyn Publications, 1990.

Jordan, Wynne. "A Conversation With Dennis Elwell." *The Mountain Astrologer* (August/September 1996) P.O. Box 970, Cedar Ridge, CA 95924.

Maynard, Jim. *Calendars: Celestial Influences*. Ashland, OR: Quicksilver Productions.

Ridall, Kathryn. *Channeling*. NY: Bantam Books, 1988.

Rudhyar, Dane. *Astrological Timing*. New York: Harper and Row, 1972.

Thornton, Penny. *The Forces of Destiny*. Weidenfeld and Nicolson, 1990.

Vaughan, Valerie. *Persephone is Transpluto*.

White, Michael and John Gribbin. "A Brief History of Stephen Hawking." (condensed from *Stephen Hawking: A Life in Science*) *Reader's Digest* (February 1993).

About the Author

Rosalind Thorp was born in 1936 near London, England. She immigrated to Vancouver, Canada in January 1957. She worked as the Chief Technologist and consultant in the field of Immunohematology at two Vancouver hospitals.

After beginning a family, she became interested in landscape design and established a very successful business in that field—Rosalind Thorp Landscapes, Ltd. It was during this period that she became involved in spirituality, metaphysics and environmental issues.

Her writing ranges from a thesis for the Canadian Journal of Medical Technology (April 1965) on Immunohematology to presentations as a landscape designer that included detailed drawings. She currently writes a column called "The Indigenous Gardener" for an environmental magazine.

Thorp now lives overlooking the sea on a small island in the Strait of Georgia in British Columbia.

Acknowledgements

The Essential Pattern was hand written in a time before I became computer literate. I, therefore, owe much to my daughter Anne, who with loyalty and courage, undaunted after each day at work, devoted herself to the task of entering the first draft of my manuscript into her computer; to my son-in-law, Bill Chalmers, who patiently guided my ideas and encouraged my endeavors; to my loving companion, Don Enz, for his enthusiasm and who encouraged me to clarify and simplify; to both Bill and Don for reading the final manuscript; to John Rutherford who introduced me to astrology; to Tim Lofstrom who taught me so well about computers, allowing me to prepare the final disc; to Gary and Ariane Bruendl, Don and Sheila MacKinlay, Richard Beard, Tricia and many others for their love and support; and, not least, to my publishers, Brian Crissey and Pamela Meyer.

Thank you.

Appendix

Uranus/Neptune Conjunction 1993: Interpretation

Uranus approached Neptune

Text: Underground pipelines suddenly ruptured releasing gas.
Underground pipelines (Neptune) suddenly ruptured (Uranus) releasing gas
(Neptune)
Neptune (hidden) Uranus (neutral / unexpected upset) Neptune (attempt to escape)
   Upsetting event involving something hidden.

Text: Unexpected flooding undermined houses.
Unexpected (Uranus) flooding undermined houses (Neptune)
Uranus (upsetting event) Neptune (secretly washing away)
   Upsetting event involving water.

Text: A sudden mine explosion trapped miners underground[1]
A sudden mine explosion (Uranus) trapped miners underground (Neptune)
Uranus (upsetting event) Neptune (hidden from view)
   Upsetting event concealed below the surface

Text: A train suddenly went off the tracks spilling toxic chemicals causing evacuation
of a town.
A train suddenly went off the tracks (Uranus) spilling toxic chemicals causing
evacuation of a town (Neptune).
Uranus (machinery, change) Neptune (pollution, attempting to spoil, disappearance).
   Sudden unexpected change involving pollution

   These events were first sudden and unexpected and then disruptive and
inconvenient.

   Here we see the influence of Uranus forcing Neptune to reveal unsatisfactory
situations, and the typical influence of Neptune attempting to escape or disappear
from a situation that must be faced. Westray Mine disaster enquiries are still
proceeding 12.11.96 which shows the long-lasting and far-reaching effect of Neptune.
It also shows how Uranus initiates an upset.[2]

---

1. NOTE: 26.06.97 CTV News Wei Chen reporting. After five years the cause of the Westray Mine disaster is still
not known. The next meeting will be in November 1997.

Uranus receded from Neptune

Text: Private lives were suddenly exposed.
Private lives (Neptune) were suddenly exposed (Uranus)
Neptune (pretentious images: deceptive charm, illusions of grandeur)
Uranus (sudden shattered images were shown to be false)

Other Examples: The nice neighbor was shown to be a vindictive gossip.
Not in text: The pretty woman was shown to be a thief.
The good guy was shown to be a cheat.

Release from a long unsatisfactory marriage was suddenly possible.

Here we see the long-term influence of Neptune attempting to conceal the real character traits and hiding the true nature of a marriage. As Uranus aligned and receded from Neptune hidden facts were suddenly revealed. Deception was exposed forever, as though a veil were lifted. In these examples something that had been hidden for a long time was suddenly out in the open.

The following table shows the alignments prior to the MV BRAER shipwreck and outlines the cosmic energy influences at the time of the Sumberg oil disaster.

2. Westray Mine disaster, May 9, 1992.

TABLE 1. Prevailing cosmic alignments cause global effects: shipwreck

Alignment Date	Energy Influence	Energy Principle	Effect
5.01.93			
Mars[a] opp. Neptune[b]	Mars/Neptune	activity paralyzed, connection with water, or navigation	ship ran aground
6.01.93			
Mars opp. Uranus[c]	Mars/Uranus	strain or stresses	hull under strain
	Mars/Uranus/Neptune	connection with accidents	sudden shipwreck
7.01.93			
Sun[d] semi-sextile Saturn[e]	Sun/Saturn	separation	separation from ship
7.01.93			
Sun opp. Mars	Sun/Mars	the will to live	
	Sun/Saturn/Uranus	sudden separation carried out in haste	
	Sun/Mars/Saturn/Uranus	sudden hasty separation in order to survive	crew abandoned ship
8.01.93			
Sun conj. Uranus	Sun/Uranus	upset or excitement	
8.01.93			
Sun conj. Neptune	Sun/Neptune	frailness, weakness	chaotic conditions
	Sun/Uranus/Neptune	unexpected events connected with water or navigation	
8.01.93			
Mars inconj. Saturn	Mars/Saturn	harmful or destructive energy	death
	Mars/Saturn/URANUS	violence, brute force intervention by "Providence"	violent destruction ship broke apart
8.01.93			
Sun opp. Moon[f]	Full Moon	imbalance	high tide
Moon opp. Uranus	Moon/Uranus	restlessness	
Moon opp. Neptune	Moon/Neptune	hidden fluids (oil)	
	Sun/Moon/Uranus/Neptune	fluid imbalance	sudden oil spill
12.01.93			
Mercury opp. Mars	Mercury/Mars	disputes	lawsuits
13.01.93			
Mercury semi-sextile Saturn	Mercury/Saturn	limited journeys	no more oil transportation
	Mercury/Mars/Saturn		

a. Mars (*energy*)

b. Neptune (*paralysis*)

c. Uranus (*freedom*)

d. Sun (*vitality*)

e. Saturn (*restriction*)

f. Moon (*fluids*)

Astrological Hierarchy

SYMBOLS	COSMIC BODIES	CYCLES (approx.)
⊕	EARTH	365 DAYS
☉	SUN	————
☽	MOON	28 DAYS
☿	MERCURY	88 DAYS
♀	VENUS	224.7 DAYS
♂	MARS	687 DAYS (2 YRS)
♃	JUPITER	11.86 YEARS (12 YRS)
♄	SATURN	28-30 YEARS (29 YRS)
♅	URANUS	84 YEARS
♆	NEPTUNE	165 YEARS
♇	PLUTO	248 YEARS

Formula

Fri. 26 evening[3]

Past Present & Future exist because the Earth is moving

the motion of the Earth
    spinning in orbit
may be interpreted in terms of the Earth
leaving, or continually moving away from where
it was,
The Earth moves into time
    time spaces
    space
Earth: Space = Time
(energy) +
All other cosmic bodies
also keep moving into
    space
their respective positions
(create) are patterns

Earth + Cosmic Body Arrangements	=	energy pattern
energy in space pattern	=	time
movement in time	=	past, present, future
moments in time	=	positions
	=	energy focus points in space
	=	shapes in space
positions may be viewed, examined from different points	=	perspective

(reverse) points maybe considered from positions
    This is known as perspective.
    Perspective involves Neptune
    (is in the realm of)
    Neptune allows us to look at something without being (there) present
    Perspective may be described as "A point of view."

3. printed version of handwritten channel

Glossary

The words in this glossary are used in the text with the following meaning.[1]

A

Alignment: arrangement in a line. A cosmic energy link or pathway. (SOED)

Angular Network: the invisible geometric linking among cosmic energy sources and receptors.

Ascendant: the degree of the zodiac rising at the eastern horizon of the birthplace at the moment of birth. (LEA)

Aspect: angular relationship between two cosmic bodies or important points on the zodiac; one of a set of specific angles. (LEA)

major aspects		minor aspects	
conjunction	0	semi-sextile	30
sextile	60	semi-square	45
square	90	septile	51.4
		quintile	72
trine	120	sesqui-quadrate	135
opposition	180	biquintile	144
		inconjunct	150

Astrology: the science of the stars; the parent of astronomy and, among the ancients, synonymous with it. (LEA)

Astrological Hierarchy: planetary precedence: an apparent order of rank.

C

Cosmic Body: the general term for natural objects which exist outside of the Earth.

Cyclical Interval: the duration of one complete cycle.

---

1. (SOED) Shorter Oxford English Dictionary; (LEA) Larousse Encyclopedia of Astrology.

D

Dimension: a cosmic energy definition in space. a unit of cosmic energy definition. measurable extent of any kind, as length, breadth, thickness, area, volume; measure, magnitude, size. (SOED); extension in time. (SOED)

E

Ecliptic: The sun's apparent path around the Earth, also called via solis, or the Earth's orbit as viewed from the sun; a GREAT CIRCLE used by astrologers, so named because it is on this circle that eclipses of the sun and moon occur. In the course of its APPARENT MOTION along the ecliptic, the sun passes through the twelve signs of the zodiac; one such revolution constitutes a year.

Energy Cycle: period of specific cosmic energy influence.

Energy Expression: cosmic energy interaction.

Energy Effect: cosmic energy manifestation, or the term for what happens on Earth.

Energy Influence: the prevailing cosmic energy in one's environment.

Energy Principle: a specific cosmic energy influence.

Energy Radiant: path of cosmic energy flow.

Energy Direction: energy pathway or cosmic energy links.

F

Focus Point: (energy focus point): a position to which cosmic energy is directed.

K

Karma: "In Buddhism, the sum of a person's actions in one of his successive states of existence, regarded as determining his fate in the next; hence, necessary fate or destiny, following as effect from cause."

Merge Point: a cosmic energy convergence point.

Moment: the specific shape of each expression of cosmic energy.

Mid heaven: the position of the sun at local apparent noon; also Medium Coeli, Latin for "middle of the sky." (LEA)

N

Natal Position: the position of a cosmic body in a birth chart including the degree of the ascendant and mid heaven.

O

Ontogeny: the history or science of the development of the individual being; embryology. (SOED)

P

Phylogeny: the race history of an animal or vegetable type. A pedigree showing the racial evolution of a type of organism. (SOED)

S

Sensitive Point: the position of an important degree in a natal pattern.

Source Point: position from which cosmic energy radiates.

Synchronicity: the principle of timing.

T

Time: includes all dimensions but the context and meaning differ. Time and space are one in the moment of energy expression. Without space energy cannot express itself. Energy fixes time in the moment, or defines the dimension.

Transit: the passage of a planet through a sign of the zodiac; the passage of a cosmic body over the position of a planet or important point in a natal pattern. (Larousse Encyclopedia of Astrology)

index